"An excellent reminder of our dependence on God's gracious intervention in all our endeavors. Through the story of Moses' leadership, Weber encourages us that our highest calling as leaders is to be servants for God's purposes in every circumstance. For anyone facing challenges in leadership, this book points to our need for an encounter with God's love so that we can become obedient servants for His work. I highly recommended it."

-Dr. David W. Kim, *President, University of Valley Forge*

"The Moses Manual takes you on a leadership journey that brings you face to face with the largest two obstacles of effective leadership, lack of obedience and fear. I love Laverne's quote, "Obedience in spite of fears is more valuable than obedience when we know it will be ok." Laverne shares life leadership lessons woven throughout the account of Moses' journey from Egyptian prince, to shepherd to leader of the Israelites on their journey to the Promised Land. We all are on a journey and can learn some valuable lessons from this book!"

-Liz DeFrain, *PennDel Ministry Network Women's Director*

THE MOSES MANUAL

Wilderness Walking
For Leaders

Laverne Weber

Published by Laverne Weber Ministries

Design: James J. Holden

Subject Headings:

1. Christian Spiritual Growth   2. Christian life.   3. Bible Study

4. Leadership

ISBN 978-0-9991966-4-9 (paperback)

ISBN 978-0-9991966-5-6 (ebook)

DEDICATION

With special thanks to my amazing husband, Pat, and our three wonderful children, Patrick, Heidi and Gretchen. Their encouragement has carried me through many wilderness experiences.

CONTENTS

-PROLOGUE-

They were a manipulative, self-seeking, quarrelsome lot. Their history was rife with lies and betrayal. One was even named Deceiver. Although they were a close-knit family, Deceiver's sons thought nothing of deceiving their father, selling their own brother, or cheating a daughter-in-law. But God loved them and had given their ancestor, Abraham, a promise. God keeps His promises!

Now this family grew and became comfortable as they settled in Egypt. They had good land and peace. Then life in Egypt changed. A new dynasty came into power and, with it, a new Pharaoh who turned Egypt into a place of slavery, abuse, and heartache.

So often, we do not see beyond the present. God allowed the heat to be turned up in their Egypt, not to punish, but to prepare them for His deliverance; not because He didn't care, but because He did care. He cared infinitely more than they could understand in their present. If given a choice, they might have stayed in comfortable Egypt. They may have even stayed when it wasn't so comfortable. In the end, their numbers would have diminished, and the promise given to Abraham would have failed.

Do you feel like you are content with things just as they are? Maybe you have a promise, but it seems so remote and impossible that your grip is gradually slipping. The Israelites cried out to God as the burdens of Egypt became more insufferable. They kept reminding Him of the promise. When we cry out to God, we can expect deliverance. The big question is this: *"Are we ready to be delivered from our comfort zone?"*

What promise has God given you that has yet to be fulfilled?

My father, George Hemminger, had a promise, a very definite one. When it looked impossible, he held on. When it seemed to be slipping away, he held on. And God kept that promise, and is still keeping it, even though he has gone on to his reward. You see, I am part of that promise.

God's Time Is the Right Time

At just the right time, a woman named Jochebed conceived a man-child. She and her husband, Amran, had a daughter and a three-year-old son, but there is always something exciting about a baby. This baby would be a symbol of hope and new life in their Egypt. They prepared for the birth.

Amran and Jochebed believed in God and His promise. They cried out to a God they had only heard about, but in Whom they chose to believe. Faith is always a choice, but once made, we must expect an answer. Jochebed delivered a beautiful baby boy. Despite a new edict from Pharaoh that all Jewish boy babies must be thrown into the Nile River, Jochebed sensed that this boy baby was special. Exodus 2:2 says she hid him for three months. Daily living in the fear of discovery takes great courage. This couple had the unique ability to step out of their anxious fears and move toward God's faithfulness.

The Moses Manual

It's a familiar story. A mother who realizes she can no longer hide the cries of a three-month-old. A little papyrus ark placed in the river, a place near where crocodiles often rested, hidden in the rustling reeds, awaiting an unsuspecting prey. A little girl hides and watches over her baby brother. A princess, raised to think only of her own needs, sees a crying baby boy and feels the stirring of a mother's heart. Before long, Moses is back in Jochebed's arms, but now she is raising her son to be a grandson of Pharaoh. Now her son will live!

God's plan performed by God's people produces the promise. What if Jochebed and Amran had been too fearful to sense God's leading? What if Miriam had failed in her task? What if Pharaoh's daughter had missed the basket? *"What ifs"* can consume our thoughts and hinder our actions, but if we let God direct us, we can trust that He does have a plan, a good plan!

Have you ever felt like you were in Egypt? Did it look hopeless? What promise has God given to you and to those you lead? What is He asking you to do that is beyond your natural ability? What steps do you need to take to lead those God has called you to lead?   If you are ready to step out and into the promise of God, Moses may be just the leader to give some insights to help you in your journey.

-1-

WHO ARE YOU ANYWAY?

*My frame was not hidden from you when I was made in the
secret place, when I was woven together in the depths of the
earth. Your eyes saw my unformed body; all the days ordained
for me were written in your book before one of them came to be.*
(*Psalm 139:15-16, NIV*)

God is not a God of coincidence; He is the God of the divine plan. The Lord spoke to the Psalmist, and He has the same message for you. God knew you and set you apart for a specific purpose even before He formed you. Before your first cells began to reproduce, God had His hand on you. You are uniquely called for this time and for His specific plan. You are a person of purpose. What is that purpose?

As I look back at my life experiences, I am amazed at the variety I see. Little seedlings of ability that I didn't consider valuable God nurtured and watered until they became a part of who I am. My love for digging into Biblical truths, my willingness to listen and help people with broken bodies and hearts, my thrill at watching children, and now adults, *"get"* a new idea all started when I was a child. And yet, I so struggled with my value!

We have a hard time accepting our value, or we just think we are not enough. The enemy would like to rob us of all God has for us, both in this life and in eternity. I know when I am about to minister, I hear these little whispers, *"What can you tell them that they haven't heard?"* or *"Why would they want to listen to you?"* If we do not fight those thoughts with God-thoughts, we will succumb to their deceit. We need to see the truth of God's Word and accept that we are indeed of great value to the One Who created us, Who loves us, and Who will guide us as we follow His call. If we dare to seek God for Himself and for His vision, we can move into being all He created us to be.

God ordained the birth of Moses into a family of slaves. That doesn't sound right! But listen. It was obvious from his birth that this baby was an extraordinary child. His parents knew it and took great risks to preserve him. The daughter of the wicked Pharaoh, the same despot who feared the Hebrews, the same one who decreed that all Israeli baby boys be thrown into the Nile River as crocodile food, saw this small baby boy and knew he was special. She risked her father's wrath to provide for him and finally brought him into the palace itself as her own son. I believe God enjoys seeing the enemy squirm. Only a daughter can totally wrap her father around her little finger. Only Pharaoh's daughter could have kept Moses alive, and only Pharaoh's daughter could have actually brought this child into the palace as one of Pharaoh's grandsons, possibly an heir to his throne. Only one person could have made it happen, and God put her there at the right time. He put that special love in her heart for that little Hebrew baby.

A Slave or a Prince or a Fugitive

Moses grew as a prince in Pharaoh's palace. Acts 7:22 tells us that he was educated in all the wisdom of the Egyptians and was powerful in speech and action. Here was an exemplary young man in his prime, able and ready to be a mighty leader. He had the education. He had charisma. His speech was impressive. We would look at him and say he has all it takes to be a success. But wait. In God's perspective, there was a small matter that needed some work. Maybe just a little time or instruction. Then again, maybe it wasn't such a small matter. Maybe it would take quite a bit of time and work.

Moses knew his background. He was a Hebrew. Born a slave. Apparently, he knew his birth parents. His mother had been faithful to instruct her son in his early years in God's ways and God's promises. According to Acts 7:25, Moses believed that his own people would recognize in him the fulfillment of God's promised deliverance from Egypt.

One day Moses decided to visit his people and see their situation first hand. He stepped out of his royal box and went to where those he loved were hurting. Jesus Christ did that for us when He stepped down from Heaven's majesty into a small smelly stable. He calls us to step out of our comfortable churches into a hurting world. We are children of the King of Kings, and as such, we are now divine royalty. Like Moses, we have been adopted. Like Moses, we have potential siblings that are still slaves in Egypt.

Moses had every right to be a prince. He

belonged in the house of the king of the land. But one day, Moses stepped down to where his relatives were, and he saw their suffering. His heart responded with anger at the injustice. At this point, he faced a choice. Would he be a prince of Egypt or a Hebrew slave? Would he choose earthly comforts and pleasures or suffering for Christ? (Hebrews 11:25-26)

In a flame of passion, he killed an Egyptian to protect a Hebrew slave. He took a risk, and then he was rejected by the very ones he tried to rescue. Aware that the word was out and the Hebrews were not going to cover for him, Moses fled. What else could he do?

Sometimes we are so caught off guard when we know we are being led by God to minister to a certain group of people, only to find that they are not ready to receive us. Maybe we have been trained in the best schools. Maybe we have been lauded by our peers and praised by our instructors. We know that we have the ability. Why can't these people see that we are there for them?! Well, maybe, just maybe, we are not as ready as we thought we were.

Is it an identity crisis? Or all a part of God's preparation?

Losers Can Learn

Moses had the ability. The problem was he knew he had it. What he did not yet have was the humility and meekness necessary for God to get all the glory. Moses was ready to move out for God and God's people. There is, however, an advanced school of theology that is only found in the wilderness of personal failure. Maybe it involves sitting at the feet of one who is not as educated or as trained in the ways of this world as we are, but knows God in a simple and profound way.

My father was such a man. He had to leave school after sixth grade to help provide for his family. At the age of thirteen, God called him to the ministry while Dad was working in the blasting inferno of a steel mill furnace. He simply said, *"Yes."*

At only twenty-two, he left all he knew and went to the mission field. Dad never felt adequate for the ministry, but he poured his life and heart into it for Christ's sake. Despite many adventures and hardships for the Lord, his main focus before he passed away at the age of seventy-seven was that he had not sacrificed enough for the Christ Who died for him. I learned so much from this humble pioneer of missions. If I ever get close to having his heart for the ministry, his powerful prayer life, his humble devotion to the Lord, or his trust, coupled with obedience, I will feel like I have begun to follow Jesus.

Moses needed to sit under the tutelage of such a man. His name was Jethro, and he was a Midianite priest. The Midianites were descendants of Abraham through his wife, Keturah, and were also God-followers. Moses, under Jethro, would have been similar to someone with a master or doctoral degree doing an internship with a simple country preacher. But that is what was good for Moses. So, God did what was needed in the life of Moses.

A proud prince became a fugitive, leaving all his hopes and ambitions behind, and going to the most isolated wasteland he could think of. It was a very low time. There he would spend forty years seemingly forgotten by God and his own people. There he would lose his Egyptian skills and style. There he would herd sheep, marry a foreign woman, and have two sons…a pretty lowly existence from that of the prince of Egypt. As Moses spent his long days tending obstinate sheep through a desolate wilderness near a mountain called Sinai, he thought he had failed. Have you ever felt that way?

I have. I've made mistakes, ones I regret. Satan enjoys reminding us of those failures and telling us we will never be able to make a difference. God promises that He will take our weakness and use it for His glory. We must choose what voice we will believe.

Our time of personal failure is not the end. It is just the beginning of knowing our Lord in the fellowship of His suffering, His rejection, His death to self and ambition, and the new power He wants to develop within us. It is the wilderness time to be sure, but it is not a time to grieve and lose hope; rather, it is just the right time according to God's plan that was decided before we were formed in the womb of our mother.

Jesus needed to spend time in the wilderness before His earthly ministry. Paul spent some years in the wilderness preparing to be God's apostle to the Gentiles. Have you felt ready to conquer the world for Christ only to fail and find yourself in a wasteland? Then you are in good company. Lift up your head. God's promise has not changed. His hand is still on you. It is just that you must have your own wilderness experience before you can lead a congregation through their wilderness.

Moses thought his skills as an Egyptian prince prepared him to be the deliverer of the Israelite nation. While training and skill are very important in our preparation for leadership, it is not until we fail in our natural abilities that we can say, *"God, I have nothing for You to use."* When we finally give up, God smiles and nods His approval. Now He can begin to speak to us. Now we are ready to listen. And so it was that one day while Moses was watching some self-willed and rather silly sheep, God came to where Moses was. God does that. Sometimes it is at the least expected times.

Moses struggled with his identity. Do you know who you are? Have you been broken so that you are able to let go of your plans and see what the Lord is planning?

We need to prepare for our purpose, but we also must know who we are in the now. Moses was where he was! Slave, prince, shepherd in a wilderness or the leader of several million people. He did not lament his past palace life. He just did his best in the now.

-2-

WHAT IS GOD ASKING OF YOU?

While I was speaking at a mission youth camp, a young man caught my eye and that of my interpreter. Although he looked so hardened for one so young, he came forward for prayer after the service. We prayed for him several times without seeing any change in his demeanor. Then suddenly, he fell to his knees.

That morning a part of my message, a part I'd almost left out, was on David, the shepherd boy. As a child, this young man was a shepherd boy. God had given him a dream that one of his sheep separated herself from the flock, turned to him, and he heard God calling him into the ministry. The very next day, one of the sheep separated herself from the flock and turned and stared at him. It was exactly as in the dream. Then he heard God's call to serve Him.

But the enemy of our souls is also the enemy of our calling. One day a *"Christian"* uncle arrived and abused this little boy. He began to put up walls. That morning at the altar, he poured out his hurt and pain to Jesus and to us. Tears flowed slowly down his cheeks. In amazement, he touched the tears and looked at his wet hand. This was the first time he had cried in over ten years! In that encounter with the love of Jesus, God renewed a very *"dead"* vision.

Moses' vision was dead. He didn't think he was a failure; he knew it! He no longer had any expectations. He had buried them long ago on one of those days while he stood in the sweltering sun staring at his father-in-law's sheep. His dreams were gone, but God's call was alive.

Have you given up on your vision, that part of you that used to be so alive and hopeful? Is your vision dead? Do you feel that God and people have judged you? Maybe they have forgotten you? Maybe, you have judged yourself and passed sentence. Do you live out your days with a sense of empty drudgery? Have you stopped expecting things to change? Pour out your hurts and disappointments to the Lord. Feel His love. Hear His call. The young man at the youth camp came to an altar. Moses traveled the distance to the Mountain of God, Mount Horeb, also called Sinai. Both left the usual, the comfortable, not really expecting, just being there.

Will You Step Into Your Purpose?

God totally knows what you have done in the past. He knows just where you are now. And He knows how to find you.

Stop right now and give your lost dream to Jesus. Choose to forgive those who have hurt you. Let the Lord carry your pain and disappointment. Let Him heal your hurting heart and ignite that little spark in your spirit.

When God Breaks Into Our Ordinary

Even at the Mountain of God, it was just another dull day for Moses. The desert heat hung in the air, and the sheep moved slowly from one tuft of scrub grass to another. Heat makes one drowsy, but a shepherd is always alert to the sheep and the area where they feed. Moses scanned the base of the mountain. It was familiar; he'd come here often. Maybe the tranquility or the name, Mountain of God, gave him hope. Maybe here he felt there just still might be a little flicker of hope. A bush fire caught his attention.

"No wonder," he thought. *"This heat is intense."*

But the bush continued to burn, and it was not burned up. I can picture Moses rubbing his eyes and wondering if he'd been too long in the sun. Moving closer, he stared at the bush. The flame was brilliant.

> ***"I've got to get a closer look at this. I will go over and see this strange sight – why the bush does not burn up.", he said. (Exodus 3:3, NIVC)***

"Moses! Moses!"

And Moses very calmly replied, *"Here I am."*

Probably not! What was this strange sight? Who is talking? How does He know my name? I think this eighty-year-old former prince probably answered in a hushed whisper.

What do you do when God steps out of the box of your expectations and comes to you on an ordinary day? How do you respond if your vision is dead and then your name is called?

Moses started to move closer only to be stopped by the voice of God Himself, *"Take off your shoes."*

> ***Then he (God) said, "I am the God of your father, the God of Abraham, the God of Isaac and the God of Jacob." (Exodus 3:6, NIVC)***

God, the God of his father, Amram? That is personal. And the God of Abraham, and the God of Isaac, and the God of Jacob. That is eternal. This God was speaking to him. Moses hid his face.

How does one react to God? Moses reacted in awesome fear. You cannot ignore God when He comes calling your name. How will you respond?

There Are Others

God's next words were not about Moses and his suffering. Instead, the Lord's focus was His people in

Egypt. Yes, He came to Moses and called his name. God knew Moses. And God knows you. He calls your name even as you read these words. But there are others. It isn't really about us. It is about a world of people that are lost and hurting, and a God Who loved them to death, death on a cross.

I remember a time when I felt life just wasn't fair. I had my time of grumbling, and then I looked down at the coffee table where my mother-in-law had left some tracts. I picked up the one on David Livingstone. I read about his dislocated shoulder, his lack of teeth from malnutrition, the negative comments about him in England, and his passion for taking the Gospel to the Africans. As I read his comment about seeing in the distance the smoke of a thousand villages that still had not heard about Jesus, I broke. It was, and will always be, about others.

But Moses wasn't there yet. The first response he made after realizing Who was speaking was a negative one. Not only did the Pharaoh hate him, but his own people had rejected him, too. The glory and thrill of being the deliverer was in the past. This was a hard and dangerous assignment. Yet, the very Moses they had rejected was God's choice to lead them into liberty.

Moses' first excuse is *"who am I?"* I was a mighty prince, but now I am past my prime.   I am a shepherd, an old shepherd. That's all.

God must have smiled and thought to Himself, *"I know."* If God had used Moses as a prince, he would have commanded God's people, but, as a shepherd, Moses was now trained to lead God's flock. God is not looking for pompous generals; He is looking for humble, loving shepherds who will hear the call and follow the Good Shepherd. In John 21:15-17, Jesus told Simon Peter to *"Feed my lambs"* and *"Feed my sheep,"* but He also said, *"Take care of my sheep."*

Now Moses was more ready to be used from God's perspective than he had been forty years prior. God's promise that He would be with Moses was all Moses needed, but Moses did not yet know the power of his God.

I can picture God saying, *"Where are you, Moses? Take a look around. See the Mountain, my mountain?"*

And God said, "I will be with you. And this will be the sign to you that it is I who have

sent you: When you have brought the people out of Egypt, you will worship God on this mountain." (Exodus 3:12, NIVC)

What Time Is It?

God's promises may take a while to realize, but they are true for God is true. For Moses, God showed up right on time, according to eternity's clock. It was at the very end of the fortieth year. Moses would indeed bring God's people to God's Mountain to worship, and they, too, would find God's faithfulness at the very end of the fortieth year.

Where are you in God's timetable? Is it near the end of your fortieth year? When things look down, you need to look up. You are called by God, and He has a specific assignment for you. Do not allow doubts to prevent your future.

What, then, shall we say in response to these things? If God is for us, who can be against us? (Romans 8:31, NIV)

Moses hid his face from God yet dared to argue with Him. What excuses do you use to keep from stepping into the future?

What is God Asking of You?

Moses' next comment to God is a question. *"Supposing I do this?"* tells us he is not yet convinced. Humility is a good thing, but Moses had crossed from humility into fear. What held Moses back from the quick response seen in Paul on the road to Damascus or the disciples as they left all and followed Jesus? It was his fear of people's reactions, fear of his own shortcomings, fear of Egypt's power, fear of change, and fear of the cost of obedience. What are your fears?

How do Moses' fears and excuses differ from Jesus in the Garden of Gethsemane? Jesus added one little phrase that showed His true thoughts. That little phrase, *"Not My will,"* is the crux of a God-filled and focused heart. God may call us where we'd rather not go, but if we truly want His will, we will obey and trust that He will go with us and give us the power and ability we need. If God is for us, we can do all things!

EXCUSES

If a commission by an earthly king is considered an honor,
how can a commission by a Heavenly King be considered a
sacrifice? - David Livingstone [1]

And now ... drum roll, please ... God gives Moses a revelation of Himself. Moses asked, *"What shall I say is the name of the God of their fathers Who sent me?"* God replied by revealing not only His name but His power. The name He gave Moses, *"I AM THAT I AM,"* comes from a Hebrew phrase that denotes action. It implies all power, all presence, and all knowledge. The God of everything. He is all I need and all that I will need in the future. He is all-sufficient!

The power of a name – it declares who we are. It is our presentation to the world. It represents our being, our character, our reputation, our value. God called Moses by name, but when He told Moses His name, it got personal.

God continued to give Moses a message. Without a Word from God, there is no hope for a nation. Jeremiah was told that God had put His Words in his mouth. It was for the benefit of the nation. God is still looking for those who will step up to the plate and deliver the words that will change the outcome of the game of life.

God's concern was His people and the promise He'd made to their fathers. He intended to keep that promise, despite all the power of Egypt. That is integrity acted out in reality.

And even though Pharaoh himself would resist to the death of his son, the people of the land would favor the Hebrews and willingly provide them with all the finances needed for the long journey ahead. The NIV Study Bible notes call this "plunder," as in a war. It was rightfully theirs in that they had been forced into slavery and had not received wages for a long period. God was going to send His people out as victors. When God steps in, we can go from victims to victors. God makes the difference, but we must also allow Him to change our mindset so that we behave as victors.

One of the beautiful things that I've watched happen in the Victory's Journey Ministry is the change of mindset. Seeing someone who couldn't make eye contact because of their shame set free to radiate God's love is thrilling to watch! We are victorious because of Christ.

God wanted an answer, but Moses again argued. He simply didn't want to go this route, but God didn't give up. He knew, despite all of Moses' excuses, that this man was the one for the job. Is it possible that Moses' biggest struggle was with the lack of acceptance by his own people? As God answered each of the excuses Moses offered, deeper core issues were exposed.

How important is it that people believe in us? For the Israelites to be free, they must leave Egypt behind, even in their thinking. For them to leave Egypt, they must follow Moses. For us to leave our old mindset, we must leave our Egypt. For us to lead, there must be followers. It all looks so enormous....but God. God is in control, and even though there may be some tough days ahead, God will give us what we need.

What if they do not believe? Are you trying to lead a flock that does not believe in you or even want you? This flock may look like family, friends, or even a congregation. Maybe it is a flock that, for the most part, does not know or believe in your God. Remember, it is not about you or your ability to perform; it is all about your availability and flexibility to the God Who created you and them and loves you and them.

Do Your People See a Victim Or a Victor?

In the case of Moses, the great I AM took a very ordinary part of who Moses was and transformed that thing into a visual token of His power working through His chosen vessel. It was just a shepherd's staff, a tool that was constantly in Moses' hand, a tool that identified his pathetic role in life, but it became a living moving snake when Moses did what God said to do.

The obedience factor was in *"throwing"* it down. What is God asking you to throw down that is part of your identity? And, after you have thrown it down and it becomes a living thing, will you dare to pick it up again?

What we throw down, we may be asked to pick up again in a new form. God caused a dead stick to become a living snake. But a living snake is still a scary thing to pick up, even for a seasoned shepherd. Are you brave enough to grab hold of what God is doing, even if it is totally different than what you are familiar with? Moses obeyed because he recognized, even this early, the voice of God. Some things that God commands us to do may seem wrong because they do not follow our traditional understanding. But if God speaks, and we want to be His leaders, we must step out of tradition that is only tradition, and obey. Obedience is the beginning step. Without it, we will stay in the wilderness, and our people will stay in Egypt.

Then God got more personal. He went from *"What is in your hand?"* to Moses' own hand. God asked Moses to put his hand in his cloak. Moses obeyed, but he must have shuddered in horror as he took it back out and looked at the sight of his own flesh consumed with the dreaded incurable disease of leprosy.

For me, it was the possibility of a brain tumor.

But, God, in His faithfulness, gave me promises… and kept them.

Fear and doubt hover so closely when God touches our own flesh, but God took that diseased hand, restored it, and used it as a sign of His great power. The Book of Acts is not finished. The God of Moses is still alive and well and able to do more than our finite minds can imagine. *"Hide that hand, Moses. Put it back in your cloak. Don't let anyone see."* That part was probably the easy part, but when he removed his hand, it was a step of faith. And God is God. His hand was restored and as normal as the rest of his body.

The third sign could not be demonstrated because they were not near the source of the water God wanted to use. Why water from the Nile River?

The Egyptians considered the Nile River to be divine. When it was powerless and became a horror to them, it was proof of a higher deity. This time Moses did not have a question because he had experienced God's power, and he believed for himself. If God said it, that settled it.

Moses did not choose what to throw down, nor

did he choose that his hand would become a sign, nor did he choose that it would be water from the Nile River turning into blood. God chose, and God told Moses what to do. As we come near the holiness of the Almighty, we will be asked to let go of some things that are precious to us. We may see physical problems. We may have to take something in our environment and use it for God's glory. God calls, and God asks us what is in our hands. Will you *"Trust and Obey"?*

Moses' next excuse is an awareness of his personal weakness. He says he couldn't speak well in the past, and he is still slow of speech and tongue. Is this the same man referred to in Acts 7:22? There it states that **"Moses was educated in all the wisdom of the Egyptians and was powerful in speech and action."** **(NIV)**

In Jeremiah 1:6-9, we see God's prophet giving a similar excuse based on his own fear of people and his feelings of inadequacy. But, then God touches his mouth and puts His word in him. Both Moses and Jeremiah said, *"I can't"* based on their fears and their perceived limitations, but in the end, neither of them said, *"I won't"*. God did not give up. He did not consider His called ones disposable.

I Can't or I Won't

In fact, God put His finger right on the central truth. He asked Moses, *'Who gave you your mouth?'* God gives us our physical traits, and the very ones we feel are inferior are the ones God so often uses. Why is that? It is because when we are displaying a trait people know we are weak in, God's power is apparent, and He gets the glory.

I grew up as a missionary kid in Sierra Leone, West Africa. As part of the family team, I started to teach children in Sunday School and children's services under mango trees before I was even a teenager. That was comfortable, but when we went to America on furlough and I was asked to give my testimony, I froze, choked, and spluttered. It was fear. I was afraid of people's reactions. Today I am comfortable teaching and preaching. My fears changed the day I experienced the power of the Holy Spirit as I spoke.

I was 22 years old and visiting my parents one summer. Mom and Dad were so proud of their daughter being a Bible College student, especially since neither of them had been to high school. Dad asked me to preach. God dropped a complete message outline into my heart, but I said *"no"*. Because it was communion Sunday, I just didn't think I could speak. Imagine my surprise when my father preached my entire message, even though I was the only one who knew about it!

The next time he asked me I said, *"Yes"*. I dealt with my fears by convincing myself that since I knew the people at Bethel Temple I would be fine. That morning as I sat in the Sanctuary Sunday School class, a number of other missionaries and government folk from England began to come in, 16 of them. One was a Bible College president. I was not only frightened. I was terrified! When we had prayer time before the morning service I begged God to make a hole and let me fall in. I informed Him that I could not do this. But just like in Moses' case, God didn't listen to my fears. I finally prayed, *"God, I know I cannot do it. I am terrified. You are going to have to take over and the Holy Spirit is going to have to do the preaching through me."*

And that is just what God did. One young man testified that as I was speaking about Jesus, he saw

Jesus standing behind me.   That morning he accepted Christ as his Savior.   From that moment, I realized that what God asked me to do, I probably could not do, but He could and would if I stepped out in faith.   I knew I must be dependent on the power of the Holy Spirit, and that is just where God wants us.

When your children say, *"I don't want to,"*, it is frustrating.   Looking for another way is telling God that we just don't like His plan! God's anger burned against Moses when he asked God to send someone else, but God already had Aaron on his way.   God wanted to use Moses, but He already knew Moses would need an Aaron. We all need an Aaron.

And, so Moses, despite all of his excuses and the core truth that he just did not want to go, went.

It is interesting that after Moses asked his father-in-law's permission to return to Egypt, God told him the people who wanted to kill him were dead. God's timing was right because obedience in spite of fears is more valuable than obedience when we know it will be okay. God is asking for a faith that steps out into a frightening and humanly impossible situation, a situation that we really do not want to step into. Yet it is in that stepping out that we will know the awesome power and presence of the God Who said, ***"I will never leave you nor forsake you" (Hebrews 13:5, NKJV).*** In the Amplified Version, that verse states, *"...I will not, I will not, I will not in any degree leave you helpless nor forsake nor let you down (relax my hold on you)! [Assuredly not!]"*

Moses had many excuses before he obeyed. We can read about each of his *"but, Gods,"* and be amazed at his daring to argue with God. Maybe we don't argue with the Lord so blatantly, but our excuses still come into play. We may tell God we will get to know our neighbors, but we just keep so busy we don't get around to it. We may tell God we'll do a ministry, but sometimes becomes never. We may say that we will fill a need, but our own family needs overwhelm us.

Of course, Satan will try to block us from following the call. These obstacles the enemy puts in our path are real and not things we can ignore. So what is the answer?

When we know who we are in Christ, and we know His loving care, our trust factor will overtake our fear factor. When we have really felt His love, we will leave our Martha mentality in the kitchen and sit at His feet with Mary. As He speaks to us and infuses Himself into our spirit, we will hear His voice calling us to a higher obedience level. Then our obedience must be coupled with a determination that if I totally fall apart, I will still trust and obey the great I AM. While the enemy will try to make us turn back, if we obey the Lord's voice, God will see us through the test and give us a testimony.

-4-

SEND AARON, PLEASE!

Moses had a strong will. Anyone who opts to argue with God is pitting his will against God's, and that is daring. Moses was also filled with fear. What holds you back? What fears or feelings of inadequacy keep you from totally obeying that small, but persistent, voice of your loving Heavenly Father?

A combination of *"I don't want to"* and *"I can't"* prevents many potentially great people from accomplishing what was planned for them. On the other hand, many meek and lowly people with seemingly few abilities press in and accomplish great things for the Lord. How can that be possible?

As a teenager, I heard many messages on surrendering to the voice of God. It is that point when we acknowledge that God is God, and I am compelled to obey Him totally, even if I do not think what He is asking me to do is possible. As we do this, we release the principle of the talents. By using what is in our hands, we release God to develop new talents and abilities in us. He grows us, and things we never imagined, things we never considered, become experience. It all starts with surrender. At what point did Moses surrender? At what point did Moses give up on his perspective and decide to do what God asked of him?

God spoke to Moses. Moses knew it was God and, despite all of his excuses and downright resistance to God's call, Moses left the place of his divine encounter a different man. God was no longer the God of his fathers; God was the God of Moses.

Simple surrender, followed by taking the first step of obedience, will unlock the door to your divine destiny. And, after you have taken your first step, God will put your fears and insecurities into His perspective. He knows you can do all He asks you to do.

And Aaron Is On the Way

Aaron, older than Moses by three years and raised by the same godly parents, seemed to already have an awareness of God and the ability to hear His voice. We so often look at the figure in the limelight and forget that for every person in the foreground, there are many behind the scenes. Aaron would not be the key leader, but, without him, Moses would have surely struggled, and possibly failed.

Aaron was going to stand by Moses in a number of difficult situations. He would help him present God's message to the people and to Pharaoh. He would also become the first High Priest, the man who went to God on behalf of the people. If you have such a person in your life, you are truly blessed!

Although not a Moses, Aaron was just as chosen and special to God and God's purpose. He would have his weaknesses and his failures, but his life would be anointed, and he and his children would make a difference. Maybe his call wasn't all that exciting (after all, a burning bush that speaks is definitely unique), but it was clear and specific. And, most important of all, Aaron simply obeyed.

As he was going towards Moses, Moses was coming towards him. What a coincidence, or was it? How often do we see God at work and think it is just a coincidence? However, if we truly believe in an Almighty, All-knowing God, we must recognize His powerful hand at work in the smallest God-incidents! And where did Moses and Aaron "run into" each other? There at the base of the great Mountain of God, Mount Sinai, the two brothers met, kissed, and shared what God was doing. Forty years earlier, they'd thought they were ready for this assignment. Now, older and humbler, God declared they were ready.

Together they entered Egypt. Together they called for the elders of Israel. There Aaron told them everything God had spoken to Moses and also performed the miraculous signs for the people to see. This time the people believed. This time they accepted Moses as the deliverer sent from God. When God is with us, and the time is right, we can expect God to unlock the gate to hearts.

And what Moses could not do alone, he and Aaron could do together. Have you joined up with an Aaron? I cannot begin to express the valuable role that my "Aaron" has carried in my ministry. The truth is we are not intended to be loners. We need others in the Body of Christ to help hold us up in difficult days. Aaron continued to be that person for Moses.

Aaron was able to be there for him at a time when his arms were too weak to keep holding them up...and the battle depended on it. Aaron was there when rejections came and there as they learned to worship on a higher level. Find an Aaron, or as with Paul, a Barnabas, and you will be strengthened in your ministry.

-5-

FOCUSED FAITH PRODUCES COURAGE

Did you ever get an assignment from God that looked hard, but when you realized it really was going to be hard, you were caught a bit off guard? Several years ago, the Lord impressed me that I would have to go where I did not want to go in my life's journey, but I was not to fear. He would be with me. I thanked the Lord for preparing me and for the many confirmations that this was indeed His word to me.

However, when in one year, we faced our son's two open-heart surgeries, our one daughter's two accidents, one in which we drove an hour and a half to Philadelphia not knowing what we would find when we got there, our other daughter's health concerns, my husband's diagnosis of a heart arrhythmia and later of an esophageal disease, my mother's death, and even our cat's death, I felt stunned. *"Why, God,"* I asked, and so did Moses.

I am so glad that God understands our sorry grasp of His infinite wisdom and power in our lives. Just as we can accept it when our children ask the *"why"* questions (even though we may want to scream if we hear that word one more time!), God understands our desire to figure it all out. He made us!

Moses and Aaron arrived in Egypt. They talked to the Hebrew elders, and the people were responsive. It was a great meeting filled with joy and worship. Everyone left on a high. Things had changed. Instead of rejection, Moses was accepted. What a good feeling it is when the people God has called you to receive you with gladness! Moses must have felt so encouraged. Sometimes in a moment like this, we begin to feel that the battle is over. God knows when we need an encouraging experience, but even at these times, our focus must be on the Lord. Jesus could have been swayed by the people who saw His miracles and believed in His name, but His reaction to them is interesting.

> *But Jesus would not entrust himself to them, for he knew all men. He did not need man's testimony about man, for he knew what was in a man.* **(John 2:24-25, NIVC)**

We must get to the point where we trust and obey God; understanding that people and their view of us will change. God never changes, and if He has called us to a specific ministry position, that is what we are to do. God will be with us.

It Wasn't Supposed To Be Like This

God's leaders were on track. They were walking in obedience. They were expecting an *"I will not"* from Pharaoh, and that is exactly what they got. I'm sure they thought they were prepared because God told them Pharaoh would refuse to let the people go. I'm just as sure they were not expecting it to get as bad as it did. God was still in control, but at this point, it looked like Pharaoh was in control. When we see the world's system looking so successful when things are not going as we were so sure they would, what do we do?

Moses and Aaron gave Pharaoh God's message.

But Pharaoh was furious. He gave a new command that the Israelites must not only keep up with their brick-making; they must supply their own straw. It was the last straw!

The Egyptian slave drivers beat the Israelite foremen as the quotas were not met. Human nature, being what it is, people will follow a leader as long as everything is going well, and the benefits are obvious. When trouble and hardships come, people get upset with their leaders. These Hebrew foremen found Moses and Aaron as they left Pharaoh's presence. Feeling helpless and angry, they lashed out at the two that were sent from God to bring them deliverance.

> *... they said, "May the Lord look upon you and judge you! You have made us a stench to Pharaoh and his officials and have put a sword in their hand to kill us." (Exodus 5:21, NIVC)*

Who were they really angry with? When we get a promise from God, it does not mean the journey from where we are to the fulfillment of that promise will be easy. Yet, when things seem to be going wrong, a common first reaction is anger and frustration. When people feel they are helpless, there is a need to control something else. Attacking those in leadership is a form of venting personal pain. The anger was partly at Moses and Aaron as God's spokesmen, but it was primarily at God Who allowed them to feel hope and then did not prevent a worst-case scenario.

Where was their faith? Where is ours when we feel God has promised us something, and it looks like it just is not happening? In fact, it looks even worse. Maybe we are tempted to tell God we wished He'd just leave us alone. How does a shepherd handle such a flock?

Look at the reaction Moses had. He felt the pain and frustration of his new flock. He struggled, too. How could a loving, caring God do this?

Faith or Assumption

Faith that is not tested is not really faith; it is an assumption. Can we stand in the storm? Do we at least know where to run? Moses did the right thing.

When the questions come, and they will, the best place to take them is to the Lord. When the stresses, hurts, failures, and rejections are too big for us, then we are to follow Peter's admonition and cast them on Christ. (I Peter 5:7). And Peter says very simply that we can do this because Jesus Christ cares for us.

Moses simply did not understand. It wasn't the way he expected. His frustration comes through very clearly as he demands an answer from the Lord, "Is this why You sent me?" He accuses God of not keeping His promise. Have you ever felt like Moses? Have you tried to encourage someone who was already hurting and then stood helplessly by while things got worse? It is at times like that that we are tempted to doubt the promises of God. Yet Peter also reminds us that God is not a God Who is slack concerning His promises. It is at these times when we must choose; the facts that we see or the faith in things not yet seen. When everything is going smoothly, it is an easy choice, but when we are in the middle of howling winds and crashing waves, and we cannot see over those waves, then it becomes faith, tested faith.

Think about a time when your faith was tested. How did God help you get over that hurdle?

Focused Faith; Intentional Courage

Moses knew what to do, and after he poured out his frustration and disappointment with God, he listened. Sometimes we just do the first part. We vent and walk away while God is trying to tell us something that will restore our faith and help us gain His perspective.

God reminded Moses that He had revealed Himself to Abraham, Isaac, and Jacob as the Almighty God, but now He was opening a new page in history. It was the beginning of the revelation of Himself as the Lord, or Jehovah, the redemptive name of God. He would indeed deliver His people. He had not forgotten. He would keep His promise to Moses. This would be the story of the redemption of the people of Israel, a type that would enable generations as yet unborn to better understand the redemption of all of mankind to be made possible by the Son of God Himself, Jesus Christ, our Deliverer!

This was bigger than Moses or anything Moses could comprehend. He went back to the Israelites with God's answer, but this time their response was not positive. They simply did not listen or receive the promises because they were too discouraged! In the middle of a battle, it is hard to see ahead, but if we can remember God sees the whole picture and our obedience will affect generations to come, we can move forward with renewed courage.

Without faith showing itself in courage, we will not make it through the wilderness, but with faith in God, we can have the courage, and we can win the battles ahead.

Courage is obeying God when you know there will be negative responses. It's great to have courage, but it is not something we can carry around in our pocket, and it is not something we will know we have until we need it. Did you ever preach a message your people did not want to hear? Did you ever witness to someone who wasn't interested? Did you ever go to approach someone in love to address sin only to have them reject you and make accusations against you?

We faced that storm when we found out about someone in the church who was forcing another person to commit sin. That very Sunday, this person started a petition to remove my husband because he was not spiritually sensitive. What do you say? You go to the Lord! And you keep going.

Focused Faith Produces Courage

The plagues came. Time and again, Pharaoh resisted God's command. God gave the final warning!

So Moses said, "This is what the Lord says: 'About midnight I will go throughout Egypt.

5Every firstborn son in Egypt will die, from the firstborn son of Pharaoh, who sits on the throne, to the firstborn son of the slave girl, who is at her hand mill, and all the firstborn of the cattle as well.

6There will be loud wailing throughout Egypt--worse than there has ever been or ever will be again.

7But among the Israelites not a dog will bark at any man or animal.' Then you will know that the Lord makes a distinction between Egypt and Israel.

8All these officials of yours will come to me, bowing down before me and saying, 'Go, you and all the people who follow you!' After that I will leave."

Then Moses, hot with anger, left Pharaoh. (Exodus 11:4-8, NIVC)

The Moses Manual

Moses is no longer shaking and overcome with fear. His answer is full of authority. What changed the frightened Moses to God's man who could shrug off the king's threats? What made him the man who could tell the Egyptian king what he would do, and when? The more you are in communication with God, the more you are used of God, the more you will believe God. Faith that produces small miracles will begin to believe for larger miracles. While God was showing His power to Pharaoh, the Egyptians, and the Israelites, He was also showing Moses He could be trusted...and Moses was learning.

-6-

PEOPLE CAN BE FRIGHTENING

In Exodus 12:1, God told Moses and Aaron that the month they were in was to become the first month on their calendar. From this point on, there was to be a new agenda to life. There are seasons of life when God calls us to new beginnings. God gave Moses His instructions for a fresh start for His people, and Moses called the elders and told them what God said.

How do you think Moses felt as he called this meeting with the elders of his people? It was the first meeting since he'd faced their anger and frustration after Pharaoh made their workload even more unbearable by not providing straw for the brick making. How would they respond to him, to God, to God's Word? There are times when God gives us a word for someone or for our flock, and after we obey, it looks like everything gets worse. It is still God's message, and our responsibility is to do what the King of Kings commands. Moses had more courage now with Pharaoh, but this was his own people. This was a challenging task. How would they react?

I remember a few years back when God gave me what I felt was a very strong word for our church membership. In the prior year, the congregation had voted against changing the church's name, something God had really impressed on my husband to do. The word God gave me to share was about loving where we were more than obeying God. If we did not obey, we were in danger of letting God pass us by.

I told God I would give the message, but He would need to have my husband ask me to say something. To that point, I had never given a business meeting devotional. As the meeting time drew closer, I felt this message becoming more intense in my spirit. I did not want God to pass our church by. I knew that would mean death to the promises He had given us of a future revival. But I also feared people's reactions. Some might think it was a set-up. Others might think I was harsh. Maybe it would be better if I didn't have to give it. I struggled in my personal prayer times but finally realized if my husband didn't ask me, I wouldn't have to do it. After all, that had been the way I'd prayed. The business meeting day got closer. I was just getting used to the idea that I was off the hook when Pat asked me to do the devotional. How do you say *"no"* when you know God has given you something to say?

With a mixture of nerves and anointing, I obeyed God and delivered His message. No one spoke when I was finished. The change of name passed.

I don't understand why that name change was so important in God's eyes, other than it was a matter of trusting Him and the pastor God had placed in the church. Maybe it had to do with learning simple obedience. Maybe the new name, Faith Community Assembly of God, would become who we were in the future. Whatever the reason, God used me despite my lack of courage, and yet, maybe courage isn't really courage unless you are afraid.

Will People Respond or React

Would the Israelites listen to Moses and Aaron and their message from God? Would they follow through with obedience or would they choose to stay in the security of the lifestyle that was familiar? We have a message to give, but we don't know how people will respond or react. It is still our responsibility to give the message. Each individual is responsible before God for how they respond or react to that message. Some want out of *"Egypt,"* but they know it will involve changes, and change can be uncomfortable. Change takes faith and obedience. It involves moving out from the old and into the new. Some folks don't want to pay the price for those changes to happen, but the Lord says in Isaiah 43:19, ***"See, I am doing a new thing! Now it springs up; do you not perceive it? I am making a way in the desert and streams in the wasteland." (NIVC)***

"God doesn't call us to be comfortable. He calls us to trust Him so completely that we are unafraid to put ourselves in situations where we will be in trouble if He doesn't come through." – Francis Chan [2]

God will make a way for us when it looks the most impossible. He is ready to move. Are we ready to move with Him? If we are ready to move out, He will also be our covering.

The death angel was about to pass by Egypt killing the first-born. It sounds so harsh, but God always has a way of escape. Those whose homes and hearts were covered by the blood would be spared.

By now, God's chosen people had seen Him at work, and their hearts were open to God's directives. When Moses spoke, they listened. They worshipped and acknowledged the Lord and His message. Then they obeyed. The blood of the Passover lamb, placed on the doorposts of their homes, protected the believers.

Jesus Christ is our Passover Lamb. He came in all the perfection of divine holiness and walked this earth's dusty paths as one of us, yet He did not sin. Yeast represents sin. Part of the Passover ceremony involves three pieces of unleavened (yeastless) bread. One of the ceremonial steps is that the middle piece of this bread, which has a pierced appearance, is wrapped in a white napkin and hidden for a while. Jesus, the Holy Son of God, was pierced and shed His blood for us. He was wrapped in a death shroud and buried (hidden) for three days. He took my place and yours just as the Passover Lamb died so the first-born in the house could live. As we believe in His Name, we are covered and protected from eternal death, a very real place called Hell.

Jesus came to bring us abundant, victorious living. It is our choice. Are you ready to move out of Egypt? God has a good plan. Just because we don't see it yet is not reason to doubt. It is a time for faith!

> *"For I know the plans I have for you," declares the Lord, "plans to prosper you and not to harm you, plans to give you hope and a future. Then you will call upon me and come and pray to me, and I will listen to you. You will seek me and find me when you seek me with all your heart."*
> *(Jeremiah 29:11-13, NIVC)*

God's people obeyed, and God's deliverance came suddenly. It was night. It was dark. There was wailing in the background. So often, God's deliverance comes at the time when everything around us looks dark, and the people around us are hopeless. That deliverance comes to those who are ready and prepared.

Leaving Egypt is more than believing. It is preparation to move forward and a will to leave Egypt behind. For the congregation, it was a new beginning with a new month, highlighted by new ceremonies to help them remember all God was doing for them.

But What About Moses?

Forty years earlier, Moses fled from disgrace and rejection and fear for his very life. To obey God and bring deliverance to his people, Moses had to reenter Egypt. That involved dealing with his past fears and rejection. It meant confronting the people who represented those hard times. It meant delivering God's message to them!

Are there shadows in your past that you have tried to forget? Are there people and pains that pushed you out of your comfort zone and placed you on the backside of a wilderness? How long have you been in that wilderness?

Do you remember where Moses met God? Even in his wilderness, Moses apparently felt compelled to go to the base of the Mountain of God. There God appeared to him in a burning bush that was not consumed. There he met the GREAT I AM. There he received his commission with God's promise of deliverance and a future. Hebrews 11:27 tells us Moses functioned as though he could see the invisible God. He had an incredible one-on-one relationship with the Lord!

If you want to be all God plans for you to be, you must seek the Mountain of God, that private place where you are open to God meeting you in a supernatural way, where you are open to His commission for your future. Then you may be told to go back and face your Egypt. That may seem overwhelming until we think about the difference in Moses when he tried to deliver his people his way, and when he did it in obedience to God's call. Also, notice that when God asked him to go back to Egypt, Moses was in a relationship with God, listening to His voice, and walking in His presence. The very things that so frightened Moses and made him feel inadequate he could face now because God was with him.

And you may have to release some old dreams to make room for some God dreams!

People Can Be Frightening

Victory Parade

As I have ministered to people with painful pasts, I have learned one thing; God, in His great love, will be with you when He calls you to face your past. Whatever you have to deal with, He will put you in a safe place and a safe time, lovingly watching over your every step. That very thing you have feared the most may be your doorway to a new beginning. And it isn't only about you. God called Moses to deliver God's people. Moses obeyed that call. He was just the vessel God used to set a nation free, but as he obeyed, Moses gained confidence and found his own new beginning. With each plague and with each miraculous showing of God's power working through him, Moses got bolder. As we surrender to the Lord and become His vessel to use as He sees fit, we will see more answers to prayer. We will experience the joy of being used by God in the supernatural working out of His plans. When we obey what we feel God is impressing us to do, we will grow in God ourselves and have more faith to believe for the seemingly impossible.

And God doesn't just deliver us. I believe it pleases our wonderful Heavenly Father to deliver us in style. Satan is called the accuser of the brethren because he accuses God's people day and night (Revelation 12:10). How do you feel as a parent when you know your child is trying hard to do well, and someone accuses them of something? How do you think God feels when Satan accuses you to Him? Personally, I think God decides right then to show Satan how much He loves you!

Look at Exodus 12:35-38. In this passage, the Egyptians gave the Israelites all the gold, silver, and clothing they asked for. Without fighting a battle themselves, they totally plundered, totally stripped the Egyptians of their wealth, and the Egyptians were glad to bless them! Comparing the six hundred thousand men mentioned in Exodus 12:37 to the tally lists of future censuses, we must estimate that several million Israelites left Egypt that night. According to verse fifty-one, they moved out in order according to their divisions. Not only that, but a multitude of people also followed them out of Egypt, choosing to go with them and the God in whose power they now believed.

It is time to leave Egypt, but for Moses, who ran away, that may mean you have to dare to reenter

Egypt first. If you obey God's call to bring about His deliverance, He will bless you beyond your greatest imaginations.

Is there an area you have been afraid to face? Are there people you feel totally intimidated by? If God is for you, no man can stand against you, no power can defeat you, and no situation can stop you. You belong to God. You are a victor, not a victim. All the power of the Almighty God is available as you step out of your comfort zone to fulfill God's call on your life. As you obey God, and as you focus on ministering to people Christ loves, you will find that the Holy Spirit will enable you to be powerful in word and deed. You can be a Moses to your world!

God's Way or Mine?

Everyone knew the shortest way to Canaan, the Promised Land, was through the Philistine territory. Everyone knew that was the best way. So often, we just know the best way to do something. It is hard to accept God's plan when it just does not seem logical. It is hard to do the thing which seems to be negative. It is just hard to adjust our human thinking to God's higher perspective. But if we trust and do as we are led to do, we will eventually see the reason and recognize God's wisdom.

Exodus 13:17 lets us know that even though the Israelites were armed for war and even though they felt confident in their ability, God knew that facing war might cause them to run back to Egypt. War is frightening.

Coming out of Egypt, we may feel we can face anything, and then we are caught off guard by seemingly small obstacles. Egypt was the biggest nation the children of God were to face, but God did that battle for them. Facing actual war, even with smaller enemies, might be too big for them so early in their new life. God knew they were just not ready.

I have, at times, told God I was ready to face something only to realize later that I was not as ready as I thought I was. What a relief to know our God knows what we can handle and does not take us on the road where those trials we cannot handle lurk. He leads us instead on paths that may seem impossible, but where we simply must trust Him to deliver us. AS we trust, we will indeed see His glory.

-7-

FAIL OR GO FORWARD

Although the shortest route to Canaan was north into Philistine territory, God chose a different route. He led them on a detour, a long one, but they were on their way! What could go wrong?

For Moses, it must have been an incredible high to watch this mighty throng of believers moving out of Egypt. Can you imagine leading a post-revival congregation of several million?! And then, to see the cloud of God's glory or the pillar of fire twenty-four-seven! There was excitement in the camp. From Moses to the youngest child, the feeling of liberty and new beginnings was intoxicating.

Then God told Moses to turn the congregation around and go back and camp right by the sea.

According to Oswald T. Allis in *"God Spake By Moses,"* [1] this put the Israelites right between the Red Sea and the mountains to the west. While we do not totally know the topography of the land, it appears that God took them from a fairly safe area to a type of cul-de-sac where they looked confused and vulnerable to the Egyptian army.

Have you been there? Have you felt that maybe God is not all that you thought He was? Have you doubted His wisdom when you felt trapped?

Have you felt confident that God was leading you only to have everything appear to go wrong (notice the word *"appear"*)? How strong is your trust factor at such a time?

But God does know what is going on, and He does have a plan, a good one. Exodus 14:1-4 is an account of God telling Moses what He plans to do. No secrets. Pharaoh will think the Israelites are confused and will pursue them, but God would be ready, and He would get the glory and be acknowledged by the Egyptians who had so resisted Him. God doesn't always tell us exactly what He is going to do, but the outcome is the same. The enemy may try his best to frighten and discomfort us, but if we follow our God, we will see His salvation, and He will get the glory.

Pharaoh did just as God said. More concerned with the loss of workers than God or the welfare of his country, Pharaoh prepared his chariots. He took six hundred of the best chariots, and all the other chariots, all his horsemen and troops, and pursued this multitude of former slaves.

True, they were former slaves, but now they were marching in confidence into a new life. The enemy hates it when God sets someone free. That part we can understand, but why does God allow people who have been set free to get caught in a cul-de-sac with no possible way of escape? Why did he let the Israelites get into such a situation? Have you ever prayed about something, seen what looked like a wonderful answer to prayer, expected God to lead you into more great things, only to be faced with a dead end that looked hopeless?

My life preparation was to be a missionary nurse. God called me into the ministry when I was fifteen. I assumed that meant missions because it was what I knew and because I felt such a love for the people of Sierra Leone. Nursing was always a desire. I did all I knew to do to prepare, and then I applied for a missionary appointment. I was turned down.

To say I was in shock was an understatement. I felt like my life was turned upside down. At the time, I was the 3-11 nursing supervisor of a large hospital. I had several career opportunities open to me, but my heart cried for ministry. I knew I'd never be happy unless I was where God led me. The next summer, I was able to speak with David Womack, a missionary leader. He helped me to release my dreams to God and trust Him to guide me on a daily basis. (I was able to return to Sierra Leone in 2009 to minister☺.)

Up to this point, the Israelites were *"marching out boldly"* (Exodus 14:8). Their expectations were high, and their faith was great. It was a wonderful life!

Then they looked around at their surroundings and spotted the massive Egyptian army bearing down on them in an enormous cloud of dust. Terror replaced bold faith; panic ruled instead of joy. The slave mentality returned. They felt the old sense of being vulnerable again. Egypt was so large. Pharaoh was so powerful. They cried out to God in their anguish.

> *"Was it because there were no graves in Egypt that you brought us to the desert to die? What have you done to us by bringing us out of Egypt? Didn't we say to you in Egypt, 'Leave us alone; let us serve the Egyptians'? It would have been better for us to serve the Egyptians than to die in the desert!" (Exodus 14:11-12, NIVC)*

Scared people can do hurtful things. Just hours before, Moses was their wonderful leader, a mighty man of God, but now faced with difficulties bigger than their faith, Moses was the source of their troubles. What do you do when you are the Moses-person? How do you face these people? What do you believe about God as you look at the destructive forces around you, tearing you down and threatening the future of those you lead?

We need to fight against fear as people and as leaders. God's Word is filled with the admonition, *"do not fear."* I have heard that the phrase, *"do not fear"* appears three hundred and sixty-six times in the Bible: one for every day of the year plus a spare for leap years.

Fear Defeats Purpose

Why are we not to fear? Fear defeats purpose. It paralyzes bold believers and reduces them to trembling slaves. Focusing on the situation causes us to cry out in terror, and as soon as we do, hopelessness creeps into our spirits and fills us with a chilling dread. We are unable to lift our heads. We are unable to speak out or move out.

Moses answered in Exodus 14:13 and 14:

> *"Do not be afraid. Stand firm and you will see the deliverance the Lord will bring you today. The Egyptians you see today you will never see again. The Lord will fight for you; you need only to be still." (NIVC)*

Live In Forward Gear

Despite his brave words, Moses apparently cried out to God because God responded to him, *"Why are you crying out to me? Tell the Israelites to move on"*. Those are power-filled words. When there is no place to go, move on. When the enemy is coming up behind you and the sea is in front of you, move on. When it is humanly impossible, God is ready to do a miracle, and He says, *"Move on"*! Can you dare to do what God says to do?

I've learned that the enemy often attacks me physically as I am about to preach or share God's Word. I could ask someone else to take my place and go curl up in my bed, but I have learned if I pray and go forward, the symptoms will be gone almost as soon as I start to speak. As we grow in the Lord, we begin to recognize certain enemy strategies. We also learn how to pray and keep moving.

The children of Israel and their leader needed to pull their gaze away from the terror thundering down upon them. Even though they couldn't see a way out of their predicament, God had a plan, and it was powerful!

Moses, Stretch Out Your Hand…and Your Faith

God told Moses to raise his staff and stretch out his hand over the Red Sea to divide it. Moses, acting on God's behalf, was faced with a choice. What if nothing happened? What if he looked like a fool? Sometimes God drops a thought in our hearts to do something unusual, and we hold back because of fear of people and their opinions. But Moses had already seen what God could do.

Alta lived with almost constant pain. She had Tic Douloureux, or trigeminal neuralgia, a severe, stabbing pain on one side of the face. It is considered one of the most painful conditions to affect people. She was a kind, highly educated woman who was a great blessing to our family and to our church. But for thirty-eight years, she suffered much from this relentless disease.

It was a Sunday night, and as I sat at the organ, the Lord spoke into my spirit that if the pastor and elders gathered around Alta and prayed, He would heal her. Sounds great, but just that morning, a guest speaker had warned us against saying, *"God Said."* After all, we must be careful of presuming on God!

I wrestled with this. What if it was my imagination? What if I wasn't really hearing from God, but I sensed God was saying, *"Now!"*. I blurted out the message, and the leaders gathered around Alta. And God did the healing!!! Every week for months, that precious lady approached us to tell us how many days she had been pain-free.

Will we dare stretch beyond the explainable into that place where we can hear and see His hand at work?

At this point, the Angel of the Lord moved. Instead of the pillar of cloud being in front of them, it was now behind them, giving light to the children of God and dense darkness to the children of the enemy. Our God is a protecting wall that the enemy cannot penetrate without permission. While God gives His own people light to see the way to blessing, the enemy will be confused by a darkness that will affect their ability to see and understand what is happening. God's people were definitely not in the dark.

Notice the time sequence. All night long, the Lord drove the water back into walls and kept it there. The several million Israelites walked through carrying their belongings. That would take some time. The Egyptians pursued them right into this highway.

Then God looked down from the pillar of fire and cloud, His very present presence, and said, *"That's the end of the road, Enemy!"* During the last watch of the same night, God caused the Egyptian chariot wheels to get clogged in the sand and come off. The Egyptians realized God was against them again and turned to flee, but it was too late. In obedience to God, Moses looked back and stretched his hand over the divided sea. With a mighty crash, the two walls of water collided, totally covering all of the Egyptian army that had followed the Israelites into the sea. It was only just daybreak.

Moses, once again their trusted shepherd, led his congregation in a song of praise to the Lord. Can you imagine the sound of that choir filling the crisp morning air? The remnant of the Egyptian army still on the far side of the Red Sea, heard in stunned amazement. Moses' sister, Miriam, took her tambourine and sang the refrain. The women followed her, shaking their tambourines and dancing. What a service!

Leader, caught in the spirit of discouragement and defeat, God has a boulevard through the briny sea. That very area that you haven't noticed because you *"know"* even God cannot work there, look again. As the Lord speaks to your spirit, stretch your hand out, and move forward. Tell your people it is time to refocus. Tell them it is time to move out of Egypt's territory into total dependence on the Almighty. God did not bring you into your cul-de-sac to destroy you. He is so much bigger than that. He will indeed open the waters for you as you put your trust in Him.

-8-

HANDLING COMPLAINTS

Moses and his congregation saw God's mighty hand of deliverance at the Red Sea, and in that situation, God introduced them to one of His key principles. That principle was very simple: when your back is against the wall and your situation looks hopeless, when you can only see disaster, God has a plan, and it is awesome.

Singing, shouting, and waving tambourines, they turned their back on the land of Egypt. As they began their journey to the Promised Land the wilderness stretched hot and dry, but when you have just crossed a sea on dry land and seen your enemies destroyed by that same sea, you feel you can face anything. After all, if God is for us, we must be pretty special! The journey may be hard, but soon they would be in the Land of Promise! They did not know that God was about to teach them another principle. When you are in the wilderness, it can get worse.

Three days in a wilderness can make you or break you. How do we react when faced with hunger and thirst? We might cry, *"Bring it on!"* and think, *"I can do this,"* but are we really ready to face the horrors of the wilderness? Incredible winds, dust in your eyes and mouth, snakes and scorpions, and, all the time, the relentless heat is beating down on you. Goshen in Egypt was pastureland, green, and lush. What a contrast! Can it get any worse?

For the children of Israel, it got worse. Three days into the wilderness, with thirst an incredible factor, they came to water. Relief and rest, or so they thought. This lovely oasis was named Marah, or Bitter, because that is just what the water was. As thirsty as they were, this water was undrinkable. Yes, the wilderness can get worse.

Earlier I mentioned that our son had open-heart surgery for a bad aortic valve in 2003. We were only expecting one surgery. He came through it, although the surgeon told us it was a very hard operation. All was going well, and so he was transferred to the intermediate unit. We left to go back to the motel to get some lunch while he was getting settled in his new room.

Then came that nudge that I knew was from the Lord. I needed to get back to the hospital at once. As I walked into my son's room, my heart dropped. The nurse in me kicked in, and I ran out and shouted to the nurse to get the doctor. She looked at me and said I have a call in for him. I remember saying, *"STAT!"* She jumped into action. The doctor was interrupted in surgery, and Patrick was on his way to OR again.

It seems that the valve leaflet had torn and the valve was unable to pump the blood. In a few minutes, my son would have been gone.

Whether in our personal lives or in our leadership, wilderness experiences will happen. But God is faithful! In the wilderness situations, He makes a way.

Exodus 15:24 says simply, *"**so the people grumbled against Moses.**"* When you minister to people, and things get worse, they may turn on you.

How do you handle that? You are presenting godly principles that you know are true. You are praying and in communication with God for them. Yet their wilderness gets worse. You may be as stunned as they are by the situations that come against them at every turn. Your own faith may be a little shaky.

In times like this, God is still God. God had healing for those bitter waters. It was just a little miracle compared to the many He'd already done. Just a certain wood, a natural resource, nearby that changed the bitter to sweet and palatable. Just God's man crying out in prayer. When faced with grumblers and worse-than-wilderness experiences, God is listening for our cry. He is waiting to give us the directions that will help us help our people.

Note that the instruction God gave Moses did not make sense. It was not logical. It had never been done before. It was not tried and proven by someone else in ministry. But the key to the miracle was in Moses' obedience. Do you want God's answers? Expect them to be out of your normal experience range. One of the secrets to Moses' success as a pastor of such a congregation was his willingness to do what God said to do. God did the rest!

Are you facing a test in the wilderness? How should you react? What should you do? Remember, tests produce testimonies.

While people can mutter and complain, so can leaders. We must guard our lips, for when we lead others, a higher set of requirements is put upon us. As Moses sought God and saw a miracle, he also received a new revelation of God as Healer.

God's Rest Stop

After the experience of the bitter water becoming sweet, the Bible simply says, *"Then they came to Elim, where there were twelve springs and seventy palm trees, and they camped there near the water." (Exodus 15:27, NIVC)*

We would like to just come to Elim, the place of twelve springs and seventy palm trees, but God knows that it is at Marah that we are developed. But when Marah is over, God in mercy leads us to places of rest and refreshment. Elim was such a place.

There are times when we need to sit and relax; times when our bodies and our spirits need to be refreshed. One of the greatest temptations in leadership is to keep going towards the goal without caring for our personal needs. Moses and the congregation needed a break from the wilderness experience, and God graciously gave them that.

The whole Israelite congregation moved again. This time directly towards the Mountain of God. They had a divine appointment.

But, as the traveling grew harder, their memories of the horrors of slavery faded in the background. They remembered pots of meat, fresh vegetables, and delicious bread. It seemed glorious compared to this dusty desert with its howling winds and wild creatures.

The people murmured again…and again…and again. In researching these events, I find that there were at least thirteen times when they turned on Moses! They were thirsty. They were hungry. He wasn't feeding them!

Even at God's mountain, they turned and, in total rebellion, chose to worship a creature instead of the Creator. They wanted their own leader. They made accusations. And, in one situation, even his most trusted co-workers turned against him.

When the Complaints Get Worse

They thought Moses was wonderful, until they didn't.

How do you react when the whole congregation is against you? How do you handle it when those you trusted listen to the *"complainers"* and then join them?

"If your identity is found in Christ, then it matters less and less what people think of you." – Leonard I Sweet[1]

They had their own agenda, sometimes fueled by jealousy. The Israelites were just not that mature in their *"God-walk."* Each of them had a "better idea." They were very concerned with their own needs and wants, to the point that God calls it a craving, or lust, in Psalm 78:18.

God's people were dysfunctional. Is this possible? The truth is that many Christians need help in *"Laying aside every weight"* (Hebrews 12:1, KJV). Even after we accept Jesus Christ as our Savior and become His followers, we may have baggage that we need God to deal with. Unless we allow God to grow us, we will continue to act out our dysfunctional behavior. The Christian walk is the daily taking off of the old self and its attitudes and habits and putting on the new.

One of the things the ladies in Victory's Journey came up with was that in order to deal with an issue, they needed to:

- Face it

- Trace it (find where it started)

- Embrace it (admit it)

- Erase it

And God gives the grace to help us unload our junk so that we can be a blessing.

Do God's leaders always do logical things? Think of Joshua leading the army around the city of Jericho. Because the people followed him, they saw a victorious miracle. Do God's leaders always do things that are familiar? Usually not. Are God's leaders perfect? Absolutely not! Only God is perfect. It does mean that God sees the person He puts into leadership as His choice to fulfill His plan.

What a contrast between Moses and his congregation. Moses did not talk about life in the palace with its servants and fine dining. He didn't moan about the hardships of desert life. He simply followed the cloud of God's Presence, and as he did, he knew where he was headed. The congregation complained to each other at every discomfort. They forgot the pain and sorrow of babies thrown into the Nile River as crocodile food. They forgot the lashes on their backs when they were unable to meet the quota of bricks to build Pharaoh's great cities. All they remembered were onions and garlic. I like garlic, but that is a little extreme!

How can you be a Moses? What is God asking you to do to get your focus aimed correctly? What is God asking you to forget?

I can imagine Moses' reaction as he asks, *"God, what am I to do with these people?"* (Exodus 17:4, NIVC) In crying out to God, Moses went to the right Person. He asked the right question. He needed an answer, and as he listened, God directed him.

Get Away From the Shouts To Hear God's Whisper

God's first command was to get away from the people; Moses with just a few of the elders. Get away from the negative attitudes. Get away from the lack of faith. Get away from the complaining and the rebellion.

There are times when we must move away from the wrong environments if we would see the right answers. God gently led a tired and frustrated Moses to a quieter place where Moses could think clearly again.

As we get away from negative voices, we must get close to God. Repeatedly, Moses falls on his face before God. He even climbed a mountain to have that personal conversation! God spoke to Moses. Sometimes Moses interceded for the people and their sin. He reminded God of His past promises and of His reputation. On one occasion, he asked God to erase his own name from the Book if He did not forgive the people.

Moses was God's man of choice, and God trusted Moses. Moses wanted God. He wanted God to receive glory. Moses cared about the people God cared about. He was focused on following His instructions. And Moses was humble.

Now Moses was a very humble man, more humble than anyone else on the face of the earth. (Numbers 12:3, NIVC)

A principle of the kingdom of God is that He will exalt the humble, those who are not looking for recognition, to positions of leadership. When this happens there will be those who ask, *"Why wasn't I given recognition?"* Jealousy is one of those traits that will destroy us if we do not deal with it. The solution is so simple many people miss it. God created each of us with a purpose in mind. We are not all created for the same purpose. That would be boring!

If we find our purpose and serve wholeheartedly in that area we will be fulfilled and joyful, and, it will not matter where God positions others. Sadly, there will always be someone who wants the role of honor that is not given to them. As a result, attacks will come to those who God puts into leadership roles.

Jesus tells us that if they persecuted Him, they

will also persecute us. In this passage in John 15:20, what promise do we have?

> *Remember the word that I said unto you, the servant is not greater than his lord. If they have persecuted me, they will also persecute you; if they have kept my saying, they will keep yours also. (KJV)*

God chose to work through Moses. He chooses to work through leaders today. The role of a leader is not a glamorous role. It is a hard role because leaders must hear from God and also minister to the congregation. Their life is constantly being observed. Satan's goal is to discredit them and accuse them. Regardless of how careful they are, the enemy will stir up situations to try to make their ministry ineffective. It sounds discouraging, and sometimes it is very discouraging, but if God calls you to come up to the mountain of His Presence to receive His directives, there is only one answer that will bring joy and fulfillment. That answer is, *"Yes, Lord."*

The comfort given Moses in this very hard time with the congregation he loved was that he was not alone. The Angel of the Lord was there and would lead him and his people into God's promises.

God Hunger in the Trial

Moses became bold: not just a little courageous, but incredibly brazen! He was so hungry for more of God that he dared to ask the impossible of God. Earlier, we saw that Moses, Aaron, Aaron's sons, and seventy elders saw God and lived (Exodus 24:9-11). They were not supposed to be able to see God and live, but, in His mercy, God showed them a glimpse of Himself and then allowed them to live with this knowledge. For most of them, it was a special spiritual experience, but, for one man, a man who'd first met God in a personal way at a burning bush, it was more than that. For that one man, sparks of holy fire burned. Moses wanted more. He wanted something that was not available to mere mortals. With all of his heart and mind, Moses wanted to see the full glory of God!

In a rash outburst, Moses cried out to the Creator of the Universe, *"Show me Your Glory."* Moses didn't want a manifestation or a miracle; he wanted God. And because God was pleased with Moses and saw the pure desire for relationship, God made an impossible dream come true.

I think that God's heart must have thrilled at the

very idea that a human longed so passionately for an encounter with Him. After all, that is why He created man in the first place. Since that unique relationship was destroyed in the Garden of Eden, there had been precious few who even came close to communing with their God. Not only was God pleased with Moses, Moses wanted to experience God. Do you? Or are you satisfied with the *"normal"* Christian experiences?

No man could see all of the awesome glory of God and live. (His heart probably could not tolerate the adrenaline rush!) But there is something about a hungry heart that God must move to meet, and God did.

We can know God because of Jesus Christ. How deeply we know Him is our choice. Do we want to know Him a little bit, or do we really long for His presence in our lives? Mount Sinai was the mountain of experiencing God in His promises, power, and precepts. We can experience God on a daily basis. His promises are true, but we must embrace them with a faith that holds on until we receive what has been promised. His power is available to all who would give themselves completely to knowing God. His precepts, or commandments, are given to protect us from the consequences of sin and to allow us to enjoy a relationship with this awesome God. Seek Him and His Presence, and you will step into a new dimension of promise, power, and precept. Seek Him and He will let you experience His glory!

If we are truly hungry for God, we will go to Him. It is when we take the time to go to God's Mountain, the place of prayer, and His presence, that He gives us a word to give His people. God's messages are meant to be specific and powerful. We cannot possibly know the hearts of those we lead, but God does. He knows just what will break the hardest heart and give courage to the most timid soldier in His service. Moses did not have a promise or a pattern for the people to follow. God did. And so, Moses went to where he knew he would find God. He was not disappointed!

When the I AM THAT I AM met with Moses on Mount Sinai at the burning bush, He gave Moses a prophetic promise. Sometimes God speaks a promise through His Word and sometimes through other people, but it is an awesome thing when God

Himself speaks into us His plan.

There are certain times in my life when God has used Scripture to show me a piece of His plan for me. He has put desires in my heart for ministry and promised me that He would lead me into certain areas. A number of people have confirmed those promises as they spoke over my life in the power of the Holy Spirit, people who did not know me at all, or did not know the specific Scriptures or promises God gave me. At such times, I have felt overwhelmed by the almighty power of God to use people to verify the truth of His promises.

But God didn't confirm His promise through anyone else to Moses. He gave the promise, Moses held onto the promise, and God fulfilled the promise.

> *And God said, "I will be with you. And this will be the sign to you that it is I who have sent you: When you have brought the people out of Egypt, you will worship God on this mountain."* *(Exodus 3:12, NIVC)*

-9-

WHEN YOU JUST CAN'T

It's Saturday evening, and you still need to do more work on Sunday's message. On Monday, there was a pile-up on your desk that demanded your attention. On Tuesday, you had a severe migraine and couldn't focus your eyes. That evening a close friend called, and since you had not spoken for quite a while, you couldn't cut the conversation off. Besides, you wanted to chat with this friend. You also needed to talk with one of your kids about a negative report card.

Wednesday was church, and that involved extra preparation. Your desk still had urgent items covering more than one corner, and several calls came in that were emergencies. After church, you felt achy all over.

Thursday, you woke up with a horrible cold and, try as you might, you could not concentrate on that message. Bed won.

Friday was going to be the solution, but an hour into working on your outline, the phone rang. A church leader was in a family crisis and needed you right away. Of course, you said, *"Yes."* Right after that, the song leader called and had such a sore throat he couldn't sing. His normal back-up was out of town. You swallowed hard; your throat was getting pretty scratchy, too. Several more serious calls came in, and by then, it was time to get home. Dinner and the family needed your attention. Still achy, you went to bed early, intending to rise at dawn. The alarm did not go off, and you were awakened by the children fighting and the phone ringing. Company was coming to dinner on Sunday, and there were some major household projects that must be done.

Now you sit slumped over a message that sounded so powerful on Monday morning. Somewhere in the week, you lost your passion, and now you wonder if you really heard from God. After a few moments with the Lord, you dig in. For almost an hour, you work. God's Word grips your heart, and you are getting some of the enthusiasm back.

Suddenly the phone rings. One of the ladies you've been counseling has decided to try suicide. She is being rushed to the hospital. *"Can you meet her in the Emergency Room?"* You wonder as you pull on your coat if the hospital has an extra room, a nice one with padded walls.

Stress - Stress - Stress

Stress is a factor in our society, but it has really been around for a long time. Moses experienced stress with the children of Israel. It has been said that the more people you have in your congregation, the more problems there are to take care of. Can you imagine having a congregation or ministry group of two to three million people that loved you in the good times and were ready to stone you in the bad times?

Moses had another source of stress. He was trying to settle disputes and do all of the pastoral counseling himself. Some of his stress was his own fault. Lack of planning, taking on more than God intended, being consumed with the job are all going to take a toll on us emotionally, physically, and spiritually.

One day Moses had a visitor. His father-in-law, Jethro, the priest from Midian, arrived, bringing Moses' wife and sons. It was a great reunion as Moses shared all the wonderful things the Lord had and was doing for His people. Jethro was thrilled and offered up sacrifices to Jehovah.

The next day Jethro noticed Moses sitting from morning to evening as a judge before the people. Can you imagine the stress of a crowd standing around you all day, every day, waiting for your answers from the Lord?

How does that thought make you feel?

Moses had good motives. He heard from God, so he felt he needed to be there for his people. But just when we think we know how to do something, God sends someone along with a better idea. Of course, we must be sure it is a God-idea, but if it is, it may just be the incredible answer that we didn't even know to ask for.

When You Just Can't

I remember years ago when my children were young, and I was carrying quite a load at the church. At the time, my mother was very needy and called me every time she thought of something to say. I'd asked her to limit her calls to three a day, but she just didn't get it. One day I received eighteen phone calls by one o'clock in the afternoon. Some were church-related and needed attention, but many of them were from my mom. When my husband walked in the door for lunch, he found one stressed woman! I hated that telephone!

Well, God had an answer. That morning Pat was picking something up for the church and saw a great sale on answering machines. I'd always felt I had to answer every call in case it was someone needing ministry...probably the way Moses felt. But on that particular day, I realized it was my sanity or my availability. It could not be both. God cared enough about my needs and well-being to lead my husband to a great sale!

Today you may be swamped with direct messages or texts. People don't mean to overwhelm you, but the enemy does. If they know you love them and will get back when you can, they will be alright.

Maybe just a short note that says, "I can't talk right now. Is three o'clock alright?" A counselor once shared with me that people don't need an immediate answer; they need to know there will be one.

While Moses Was Reaching Out To The Congregation God Was Reaching Out To Moses

Read Jethro's advice.

> *Listen now to me and I will give you some advice, and may God be with you. You must be the people's representative before God and bring their disputes to him. ... Teach them .... select capable men ... Have them serve as judges for the people at all times, but have them bring every difficult case to you; the simple cases they can decide themselves. (Exodus 18:19-22, NIVC)*

Some areas of stress are our own doing. When his father-in-law came to see him in the wilderness, Jethro noticed Moses was trying to do it all himself. Some people do this because they feel a strong sense of obligation to God and people. Some have a need to feel important or do not trust others to do a good job. They may feel they are the only ones who will do it well. That may be true, but if we never develop our leaders, we will always have to do it all. Other people do it all because they just do not know how to delegate. Jethro, Moses' father-in-law, had a good plan.

As I get older, I am really glad for the time I took years ago to begin developing lay leaders. God has people ready and waiting to take on more responsibility. They may need some of your time in ministry, some teaching, and some hands-on demonstration, but they are also called to fulfill the work of the ministry. If you neglect them, there will be something unfulfilled in their lives. There will be people they were meant to touch that will never be reached. If, on the other hand, you take the time to develop others, you will be incredibly blessed! You cannot do it alone. Remember, it is God Who is building His church. It is His work, and He has given a variety of gifts to a variety of people to get the job done. His plan involves using the whole Body of Christ, not just one person. Ministry life involves teamwork, as every member does his or her part. A good leader must recognize that it is not just about getting a job done; it is about discipling others to disciple others.

Stress is the result of striving to carry God's load alone. It is very individualized. It can be good when our body goes into a fight or flight mode for the purpose of protection. Stress can be a signal to find new and better solutions to certain issues. Short-term stress hormonal response is normal and part of life. It helps us develop wisdom and faith and maturity and should be followed by a relaxation response as the threat passes.

On the other hand, chronic stress develops if we cannot manage our issues. Psychologists say that some people have a lower tolerance for frustration than others; others have never learned how to handle normal daily difficulties, and so everything becomes a major issue. Obviously, this can create problems if not dealt with in a healthy way. More severe problems include anxiety disorders, depression, and post-traumatic stress disorder.

There are hot reactors that blow up at the slightest problem, there are pressure cookers who just hold it all in until there is a major explosion or until they turn the stress inward and become depressed, and there are those who just become negative people with negative attitudes.

We cannot control certain stressors – the key is how we react. If Satan can overwhelm us, we will not be or do what the Lord Jesus desires us to be or do. Eventually, we will become totally inward in our focus, and God and others will not be important.

Attitudes affect how our body handles stress. If you believe it will all work together for good, you will be healthier than if you feel that things are out of control. Satan is our enemy, and he wants to have us give up. Faith in God is the bottom line that directs our reactions. Even when things have not gone as we planned them, even when it looks like our world is falling apart, God is still in charge, and He knows right where to find you. Feeling Him there is not necessary; knowing that His Word says He will never leave us is!

-10-

OVERCOMING CRITICISM

In ministry, we cannot be God! We need people to come alongside us. We need others to help carry the load and to support us in our prayers and ministry.

They tested God at Rephidim. The Amalekites attacked them at Rephidim. When we let our attitudes become negative and rebellious, we become vulnerable to attack. But God never changes.

The battle with the Amalekites is a lesson in teamwork. As Moses stood on the mountain, holding the staff of God aloft, Joshua and his army won the battle in the valley. When Moses became tired, and his arms could no longer hold their position, the enemy won.

Not all of the men were in Joshua's army, only some of them. The majority apparently stayed in the camp. In contrast, there were only two men with Moses, Aaron, and Hur. This is a picture of the battles in today's spiritual arena. Even when it seems the world is gaining ground, there are many people in God's camp, the Church of Jesus Christ. Where the battle rages, some people are heavily involved. They are doing the work that keeps the church alive; they are fighting hard, and sometimes they see victories, and sometimes the enemy strikes hard blows. It is tough out there in the middle of the fight. Some will die, some will receive injuries that leave scars, and some will survive to deal with the memories. But they are the kind of people that are so committed they will not retreat in defeat, whatever the cost.

But something more than soldiers was needed here. There are times when the battle-weary cannot do it alone. There was one that stood in the gap between God's victory and the soldiers in the valley below.

Remember, they are still camped at Rephidim, the place of testing God and murmuring against their leader. Note the humble and loving spirit of Moses. The people rejected his leadership and wanted to stone him. Yet when the attack came, Moses gave all he had to stand as an intercessor between these very people and God Almighty. Are you like Moses?

Moses stood on the mountain of intercession, and there he held up his hands and the staff of God over God's army. He was God's man, but he was only a man. The weight he carried was enormous. His hands grew heavier and heavier.

I remember seeking the baptism of the Holy Spirit and thinking I had to keep my hands straight up in order to receive God's gift. As my arms got tired, they felt heavier and heavier. Eventually, they started to go numb. Instead of worshipping God, at that point, I found myself asking God to help my arms! The focus of my attention left the Presence of God and moved to my physical discomfort.

Moses, a picture of frail humanity, could not keep his arms up. They started to fall to his sides. As his hands, and thus God's staff, dropped, the enemy prevailed. So Moses would gather all the strength he had and push his arms up again, only to find them sinking after a period of time. He could not physically carry on. True intercession is very hard work!

Better Together

God didn't send Aaron and Hur up the mountain with Moses to enjoy the scenery or watch the battle. He sent them up there to get involved with a matter of life and death for His people. Moses heard from God and went to intercede. Aaron and Hur heard from Moses and were observant enough to see a need they could help with. And they did. They were not the soldiers; they were not Moses; but without these two, the battle would have been lost. Vital to victory, they stood on each side of Moses, agreeing with him in the ministry of intercession until sunset when the enemy in the valley was defeated. They literally came alongside God's leader and picked up the load that he could not carry alone. They also looked out for a very tired Moses and provided him with a stone to sit on. Leaders need godly helpers like Aaron and Hur if they are going to truly see the victory God has promised.

I cannot thank God enough for the intercessors He has given me over the years. People I can trust.

Friends who will take the prayer call seriously. They are a vital part of the victory God gives. These people are gifts to be treasured!

We know about Aaron, but who was Hur? Josephus, the Jewish historian, says that Hur was the husband of Miriam, sister of Moses and Aaron. He's seen again when Moses goes up Mount Sinai to meet with God and leaves Aaron and Hur in charge of the Israelite congregation.

In obedience to God's directives, Moses records the event and then builds an altar. This is a place of victory, and as such, God introduces a new aspect of His character to His people. Here the Lord is called *Jehovah-nissi, The Lord is my Banner*, for here hands were lifted up to God's throne, and here under the banner of God's staff victory prevailed.

Under God, Our banner, we are winners. The battle may be fierce. The attack may be prolonged. The soldiers and intercessors may be exhausted. But we stand as one. God is our Banner, and the battle belongs to the Lord!

-11-

LOSING IT ...AND... LOSING IT

The Israelites had been wandering in the wilderness, and they came again to the Desert of Zin to the place known as Kadesh. Here Miriam died and was buried, and the entire congregation mourned for her. Moses and Aaron were still grieving the death of their sister and partner in the ministry. Their hearts were focused on their personal pain when the enemy blind-sided them with an angry attack. In other situations, the people grumbled and were upset, but in this situation, they were angry.

And the people contended with Moses, and said, Would that we had died when our brethren died [in the plague] before the

Lord! (Numbers 20:3 – Amplified Classic)

Moses and Aaron again went on their faces before the Lord. This was the right thing to do. As they sought God, His glory appeared, and He gave Moses the directions for providing water.

> *"Take the staff, and you and your brother Aaron gather the assembly together. Speak to that rock before their eyes and it will pour out its water. You will bring water out of the rock for the community so they and their livestock can drink." (Numbers 20:8 – NIVC)*

God wanted to show His power and also to show truth regarding Himself.

> *So Moses took the staff from the Lord's presence, just as he commanded him. He and Aaron gathered the assembly together in front of the rock and Moses said to them, "Listen, you rebels, must we bring you water out of this rock?" Then Moses raised his arm and struck the rock twice with his staff. Water gushed out, and the community and their livestock drank. (Numbers 20:9-11, NIVC)*

Notice what Moses said and the tone with which he spoke. We've seen Moses stressed before, but this seems to be the proverbial final straw. Instead of crying out to God for them, he calls them rebels. Obviously, the burden he felt at this moment was a size extra-large, but he forgot that it was not his burden. For the first time, he claims that he and Aaron are the ones who must meet the people's needs. Psalm 106 tells us that he spoke rashly.

When we are emotionally exhausted, we should be on guard against acting in our own strength. Moses again would have benefited from getting away and spending time with God. He was tired and sad and stressed and made a fatal blunder that would keep him from seeing the fruit of his life's work.

Then what?

God tells Moses his sins. Faith was the missing ingredient. Although Moses was a man of faith, he did not trust God to do the necessary miracle with just a spoken word. That was outside of his comfort zone. It was new and untested. When God uses us, it is wonderful, but there is a danger in depending on a method and not on the I AM THAT I AM.

The rod was a tried and true miracle-producer. Even though God said, *"Speak to the rock,"* Moses used the rod to hit it, not once, but twice. In so doing, he reacted in anger and did not honor God as holy and sanctified in the eyes of the congregation. Yet God came through, and water did indeed gush from the rock, flowing like a river to meet the needs. God will sometimes do that type of thing just because He loves His people.

There was a bigger problem with the striking of the rock than first meets the eye. This was not just one of the rocks strewn through the wasteland. Read these verses and note the identity of this rock

> *He abandoned the God who made him and rejected the Rock his Savior. (Deuteronomy 32:15, NIVC)*

> *...and that rock was Christ. (1 Cor. 10:4, NIVC)*

All Moses had to do was speak to the rock. All we have to do is to speak the Name Jesus.

We so often miss great concepts in Scripture because we do not understand the culture. When I was a little girl, and we sang, *"Jesus is a Rock in a weary land,"* I thought of a giant rock that stood out as a symbol of strength. Yes, Jesus is our Source of strength, but He is so much more!

The weary land, or wilderness, is a dry, hot place. It is a lonely place because so often the enemy convinces us that no one cares, and if they do care, they can't help us anyway. It is a place where the sun beats without mercy, where the wind whips sand and dust in your eyes, where you are thirsty for a spiritual refreshing and hungry for a Word from the Lord, but none come. Even when you do all the right things, you feel lacking and weak. It is a place of poisonous vipers aiming to destroy you and fidgety jackals anxiously pacing in anticipation of the moment you fall. It is a place where the spiritual battle rages, but your strength is almost gone. You stagger and wipe your brow. The wilderness stretches before you as an endless sea. Squinting against the glare, you whisper the Name.

Suddenly in the midst of barrenness, something catches your eye. It is large and rugged. You take a deep breath and look again. It is still there. With great effort, you begin to move in the direction of a great Rock. Shadows play around the edges of the

Rock, and you can see a hollowed out place just your size. Water trickles over its jagged edges, and at its base are the soft shades of green grass.

That Rock is Jesus. He was there all the time, but when you whispered His Name, you saw Him. He is stronger than any fortress and stands against the enemies that long to destroy you. The cleft in the Rock is a hiding place, a shelter from enemies, protection from the heat, and whipping wind; it is a quiet place where you can lay your head against the cool surface and rest. There the Living Water flows, and the very Presence of God fills your heart with peace. It doesn't matter that the storm is still raging or the sun still beating down on the already scorched earth. It doesn't matter that the enemies are still waiting or that just a short time ago, you didn't know if you could survive. You have arrived, and in the shelter of that Rock, you are safe!

God calls us to an oasis of His peace and protection in the middle of turbulence. He wants us to have the joy of drinking the Living Water poured out for us. Will you speak to the Rock in faith, or will you keep striking the Rock in your frustration and anger? Will you obey and see the Promised

Land in your own life?

Now What

But, what if you missed God's directive? What if there is a call you did not chase after? What if you failed?!

Keep going.

God's response to the anger and disobedience was clear. Moses would not lead God's people into the Promised Land. All the testings, all the dealing with this rebellious group, all the conversations with God on the mountain could not change the fact that he'd failed and, at that moment, had lost the privilege of leading his congregation into the Promised Land.

But Moses never stopped being the best Moses he could be. He kept on putting one foot in front of the other. He kept leading God's people.

Satan wants us to give up when we fall down, but God reaches out, steadies our feet, and helps us move forward. The children of Israel still needed Moses; Joshua still needed him.

Moses was an amazing man of God. He met

God. He argued with God. He agreed with God. He was focused. And, no matter what happened, he just kept moving forward in his obedience to the call. Because his heart was focused on God's purpose, he could keep going despite the personal loss. It wasn't about Moses; it was about God and God's people.

There are times when we cannot undo what has been done, but God forgives. He still loves us. He will still use us for His glory – if we keep moving on in His purpose!

-12-
PASSING THE MANTLE

It was his birthday! Moses was a hundred and twenty years old, but his eyes were not weak nor his strength gone. Yet, it was time! We must know when it is that time.

The journey was over. Forty years of traveling through the wilderness. It had truly been an impossible dream. You can't take millions of slaves out of a country, and you can't lead that many people through a wilderness without food and water. But Moses did his part, and God did His part, and the rest is history!

Years of seeing God and Moses and years of serving as Moses' aide prepared Joshua to step into those big sandals. But Moses needed to present God's new man to the congregation. He needed to affirm him as God's choice for the new season.

As far as you could see, they gathered to hear Moses give his farewell. As he proclaimed God's commandments and challenged the people to serve the Lord, he reminded them that success was theirs.

> *This day I call heaven and earth as witnesses against you that I have set before you life and death, blessings and curses. Now choose life, so that you and your children may live and that you may love the Lord your God, listen to his voice, and hold fast to him. For the Lord is your life, and he will give you many years in the land he swore to give to your fathers, Abraham, Isaac and Jacob. (Deuteronomy 30:19-20, NIVC)*

Moses passed his commission on to Joshua, encouraging him to be strong and courageous. God would be with him. Then this great old shepherd of God's flock sang a song of praise proclaiming the greatness of the God Who had led him these many years. He blessed that great multitude, the congregation for which he had given his whole life, the people whom he had loved and served.

Following the God he had come to trust completely, he walked up Mount Nebo. Moses was not alone. He walked with his tried and true Friend of forty years. I feel certain that they continued their conversation as they walked that final lap, remembering the journey, and looking ahead to the future.

For Moses, this climb would be his last. Although, because of his disobedience, he could not enter the Promised Land in his natural lifetime, the Lord gave His friend and servant Moses a special panoramic view of that Holy Land.

God, Himself, gives us the last chapter of the life of Moses, this incredible leader who knew God and who allowed himself to be used to do mighty deeds for the glory of the Lord.

> *And Moses the servant of the Lord died there in Moab, as the Lord had said.*
>
> *He (God) buried him in Moab, in the valley opposite Beth Peor, but to this day no one knows where his grave is. (Deuteronomy 34:5-6, NIVC)*

Moses did not enjoy the natural blessings of the Promised Land, but God did allow him to enter it many centuries later for a very special occasion.

About eight days after Jesus said this, he took Peter, John and James with him and went up onto a mountain to pray. As he was praying, the appearance of his face changed, and his clothes became as bright as a flash of lightning. Two men, Moses and Elijah, appeared in glorious splendor, talking with Jesus. They spoke about his departure, which he was about to bring to fulfillment at Jerusalem. Peter and his companions were very sleepy, but when they became fully awake, they saw his glory and the two men standing with him. As the men were leaving Jesus, Peter said to him, "Master, it is good for us to be here. Let us put up three shelters--one for you, one for Moses and one for Elijah." (He did not know what he was saying.)

While he was speaking, a cloud appeared and enveloped them, and they were afraid as they entered the cloud. A voice came from the cloud, saying, "This is my Son, whom I have chosen; listen to him." (Luke 9:28-35, NIVC)

Passing The Mantle

Moses had seen the Lord's glory and His provision, but in the life to come, he would see Him and speak with Him on the Mount of Transfiguration. We serve our Lord here by faith. There are times when we see a glimpse of His great glory and power, but someday we shall see Him face to face in all of His majesty. It is our hope. There is a Promised Land, and it is for all of us who refuse to quit but choose to follow our beloved Lord and Savior until He calls us to walk up the mountain into His very presence.

About The Author

 Laverne Weber is a speaker, teacher, nurse, and author of Victory's Journey and Moving On for Men. In 1993 she founded Victory's Journey Ministries as a small group healing ministry. Through the years many have found the freedom to move out of the shadows of their past into a vibrant life in Christ.

Laverne and her husband, Pat, are retired pastors and live in Pennsylvania. They have three children and four grandchildren.

Bibliography

Chapter 1

1. Livingstone, David, retrieved from
azquotes.com/quote/531164

Chapter 6

1. Chan, Francis, retrieved from azquotes.com,
Preston Sprinkle (2014). *"The Francis Chan
Collection: Crazy Love, Forgotten God, Erasing Hell,
and Multiply"*, p. 88, David Cook

Chapter 7

1. Allis, Oswald T, *"God Spake By Moses: An
Exposition of the Pentateuch"* (Nutley, New Jersey: The
Presbyterian and Reformed Publishing Company,
1972) p. 68.

Chapter 8

1. Sweet, Leonard I (2014), retrieved from
azquotes.com, *"The Well-Played Life: Why Pleasing
God Doesn't Have to Be Such Hard Work"*, p. 116,
Tyndale House Publishers, Inc.

Made in the USA
Middletown, DE
15 October 2022

12827556R00076

Contents

Introduction

Organizations around the world are facing a challenging reality: the new global standard—for those who thrive—has become flawless products, services, and experiences, delivered with no friction, 24/7/365. Never before have customers demanded so much. But for leaders who can build high performance organizations, the demands of the modern world fit right into their game plan. And for those who struggle to execute, the challenge will ultimately prove unsurmountable and the consequences dire.

For the last several years, we have been attempting to answer this one simple question: what specific behaviors enable and sustain elite levels of execution? I'm excited to share what we have learned.

The ideas you are about to explore are born of almost a decade of research, conversation, debate, and real-world cases involving hundreds of thousands of employees. We've studied scores of organizations—some household names and others quiet exemplars of what is possible: Apple, Cirque du

Soleil, Navy SEALs, Starbucks, Danaher, Clemson football, Southwest Airlines, Mayo Clinic, Zappos, and many, many more.

Our findings were clear—high performance organizations all do four things: (1) Bet on Leadership, (2) Act as One, (3) Win the Heart, and (4) Excel at Execution. These four moves *together* create remarkable organizations.

Win Every Day is the fifth installment in the High Performance Series and will focus on the fourth of these defining characteristics, the hallmark of all high performance organizations, *execution*.

For many, the ideas on the following pages will be transformational! There's just one catch. If you miss any one of the four moves, not only will execution forever be a challenge, but you'll forfeit your place among the world's great organizations. Today's execution challenges often find their energy and source in the first three moves—each represents a critical step on the journey to Excel at Execution.

One final introductory thought: this book, although simple and succinct in its final form, required a tremendous amount of work. I know that sometimes when you see a business fable, you may think a guy like me just sat down one afternoon and knocked it out—"It's just a short story." In this case, and with my other books, nothing could be further from the truth. When you finish the book, or right now, please take a moment and read the acknowledgments. We worked with scores of businesses with thousands of employees to discover, validate, and refine the truths you are about to encounter. I am forever grateful for the entire team—you will be too.

I trust this book will serve you and your organization well. It could be the last critical piece you've been searching for to release the untapped potential in your people, create real competitive advantage, and ensure your leadership legacy.

Win Every Day!

Nightmare

How did this happen?" Blake snapped.

No one wanted to respond. Then Kim Diaz, the chief marketing officer, looked at the others and said, "Well, Blake, we blew it—multiple times." She went on to explain a tragedy of errors and poor decisions involving a previously loyal customer. "The order was taken incorrectly, the shipment was late, the product was defective, and our response was incomprehensible. The result: a viral video complaint viewed by one million people."

"A million people and counting! In just twenty-four hours! What are we going to do?" Blake fumed.

"We've issued an apology to the customer and posted it on all the social platforms; we've also released the customer service representative," Kim offered.

"And what else can we do?" Blake asked.

"We don't know what else to do at the moment," Charles Jones, the head of Human Resources, said.

"This is a nightmare!" Blake said as he left the room.

~

Blake's next meeting was with Ashley Westman, the new head of Production. When he originally planned the meeting with her, he knew nothing about the firestorm they would be in today. However, he hoped she might have some fresh ideas regarding the way forward.

Still distracted by the morning's events, Blake attempted to be fully present as he greeted Ashley. "Good morning. Before we begin, I need to be sure you are up to speed on what's going on this morning."

"I think I know," she said sheepishly.

"You do?"

"Yes, sir, my phone is blowing up. All my friends know I just started working here a few months ago and they're sending me the link."

"Well, I guess the timing of our meeting is perfect." Blake attempted a smile.

"I suppose so."

"What have you discovered since our first meeting?" Blake asked.

"Well . . . I know the media attention we're receiving this morning is unprecedented, but the problem is not an outlier."

"What do you mean?"

She handed Blake a single sheet of paper reflecting the organization's recent performance.

"We are better than this," Blake said, staring at the page.

"Well, sir," Ashley responded hesitantly, "actually, the trends indicate we are not. Our execution has been slipping for several years. However, it does appear we've leveled off."

"This doesn't look healthy to me. Why do you think the numbers are flat?" Blake asked.

Ashley had not been on the job long, but she knew exactly what the chart depicted. Not wanting to be shot as the messenger, she began cautiously and spoke matter-of-factly.

"The process is in control."

"And . . ." Blake waited.

"The results we are generating are perfectly aligned with the systems, structure, and practices we have in place." She continued, "And if we make no significant changes, I can confidently predict similar outcomes in the near future."

"What if we want to get better?" Blake asked.

"We'll have to change something," Ashley said with a slight smile.

"And what should we change?"

"I'm not sure yet. But first, you and our senior leaders have a decision to make," Ashley insisted.

"What's that?"

"Are we good enough?" Ashley asked.

"What does that mean?"

"Every organization decides how great they want to be."

Every organization decides how great they want to be.

"Of course, we want to be great!" Blake said instinctively.

"Does this data look great to you?"

Blake was struck by the simplicity and directness of the question. Even without the current social media frenzy, he knew the answer was a resounding no.

"Let's talk about what great looks like," Blake said.

"First, you have to decide whom you are competing against," Ashley suggested.

"That feels like a strange place to begin, but I'll bite. We know our top five competitors globally."

"Who will our top competitors be in five years?"

"I don't know," Blake confessed.

"Okay, how good are the ones you know about today?"

"The data is a little hard to come by—some companies are privately held—but third-party estimates clearly put us ahead of them on most key metrics—sales, profitability, even quality."

"But how *good* are they?"

Blake had never thought about the question in those terms. "I guess they are mediocre," he said.

"And how good are we?"

"Better than them!" A feeling of pride engulfed Blake.

"So, it sounds like we're good—no additional action required. Right?"

Blake didn't respond.

"I have another question. What happens when a current competitor, or a start-up, outpaces us? What if they decide to up their game, and their level of execution leaves us behind? What if today's social media incident becomes a recurring event?

"I'll admit, I'm new here, but this is what I'm hearing: you say you don't like our current level of performance, but you've allowed it to continue for several years. You also acknowledge we are better than our known competition. So, I come back to my question: why change? Change is hard and costly. You need to decide. Are we good enough?"

The question struck a deep chord in Blake's soul. He knew the company was probably good enough to stay in business but not good enough for him to look in the mirror and say, "I gave my best."

Ashley waited for his response. "Sir?"

"I know the answer: we are not good enough. But the reason we have to address this has nothing to do with our competition or today's incident."

"I don't understand," Ashley admitted.

"Our current level of performance is not congru-ent with who we are, who we want to become as people—as human beings. We don't strive to do the minimum; we're not trying to just get by. Our goal should not be to just beat the competition."

"What do you want us to do?"

"I want us to do our best every day—for ourselves, our families, our customers, vendors, communities, and the world. We have so many lofty aspirations. To me, this data is in conflict with who we say we are as a brand. All that we should expect from ourselves is our very best; our current level of performance doesn't qualify as our best effort."

**I want us to do our best every day—
for ourselves, our families,
our customers, vendors,
communities, and the world.**

"What's your bottom line regarding where we stand today?" he asked.

"I think we're the best of a bad lot."

"Is that our destiny?" Blake asked.

"You get to decide."

～

After work, Blake went to a board meeting for Clint and Kristen's school. Both of his children had made great friends and excelled academically since transferring there. Blake was glad to give back by serving on the board. When he arrived, he was greeted by Paul Roker, the head of school.

"Good evening, Blake!" Paul said warmly. "How are you?"

"Really good. We're wrestling with a few issues at the office, but I guess that's why they need us," Blake chuckled.

"If we have a few minutes at the end of the meeting, I need the board's counsel on an issue."

"Okay. What's that?"

"It's about our football program," Paul said.

Blake was intrigued. As a matter of principle, the board had worked really hard not to be involved in day-to-day operations of the school—that was Paul's job.

"Okay. Anything we need to discuss before the meeting begins?"

"No, not really. I just wanted to give you a heads-up—it's clearly an off-agenda topic."

The meeting was focused, productive, and timely. As the meeting was winding down, Blake, as board chairman, looked at Paul and said, "Paul has one additional item he wants to discuss with us tonight. Paul . . ."

"Thanks, Blake. As you guys know, one of the ways you add huge value around here is all the free consulting you provide for me," he said with a smile. "Seriously, you guys have made me a better leader, and I am so thankful for your wisdom."

"Is there a specific issue on which you need some wisdom?" Margaret, the CEO of a local bank, asked, looking at her watch.

"Yes. It's about football. Well, not really. It's more of a philosophical question."

"A philosophical question about football?" Chuck, the owner of a local construction company, laughed. "Now, that's my kind of question."

Blake said, "How can we help?"

"Our football program is not awful, but it's not great either," Paul began.

Everyone nodded in agreement.

"We have won about 60 percent of our games for over a decade. Not an embarrassment but not really good."

"And what is the question?" Margaret asked.

"Is that good enough?" Paul asked.

"What?" Chuck asked.

"To win 60 percent of your games year after year," Paul clarified.

"Why do you ask?" Blake said, struck by the similarity to the conversation he had had earlier in the day with Ashley.

"I am trying to decide if we should try to improve the program—win more games."

"What brought this up?" Margaret asked.

"We've recently lost a few families who wanted their children to be part of a better football program."

"Anything else?" Blake probed.

"Yes, I realize we've set a high bar on everything we do—the academics, the arts, our service in the community. We even teach servant leadership to our kids. Heck, one of our values is 'excellence in all we do.' For me, I'm afraid it has become an integrity issue. We are not giving our best in our football program."

"Why do you need our counsel on this? Why would you not apply the same standards of excellence to football as you do to everything else?" Elizabeth, the most tenured board member and a retired school superintendent, asked.

"Two reasons: one, Coach Stone has been here a long time—he was here a decade before me. And, two, I believe we are grossly underinvesting in the program—everything from assistant coaches to the weight room. There will certainly be trade-offs . . . or budget increases."

"Do you know what you want to do?" Blake asked.

"I think I do."

"And that is?"

"Raise the bar; be true to our values and give the same level of effort in football we do everywhere else. I can't guarantee more wins, but I'll feel better about myself as a leader and our school if we do this."

Margaret said, "I don't think we need to vote on this but know you have my support. Anyone have any concerns about Paul's direction on this?"

"I'll assume silence is consent," Blake said.

Chess Not Checkers

After the meeting, all Blake could think about were the similarities between his situation and Paul's. *What are the implications of settling for less than your best?*

Back at home, Blake began to share his thoughts with his wife, Megan. After he laid out the facts of both situations, he asked, "What do you think?"

"A lot," she said, grinning.

"I need more than that," Blake insisted.

"The question of 'are we good enough?' implies that you and I, your organization, and the school have some influence over the outcome. To think we have a choice in the matter is rooted in a person's belief system. Do you believe improvement is possible?"

"I do . . . I think I do." Blake paused. "Yes, improvement is always possible."

"But improvement is *impossible* if you do what you've always done. Progress always requires change," she added.

"I know," Blake admitted.

"What else do you believe?"

"What kind of question is that?"

"A very personal one. What do you believe about your organization? What do you believe about your leadership? What do you believe you're supposed to do?" Megan asked.

"That's what I'm trying to figure out. I'm not sure when I stopped working to get better . . . or why," Blake said.

"Well, you've been focused on other things—strategy is about choices," Megan said.

"Nice try to let me off the hook." Blake flashed a huge smile. "You are correct; at the heart of strategy is the idea of trade-offs; however, your line of thinking may apply more to Paul than to me. He's not running an NFL franchise; he's leading a school. So perhaps he could strategically shift resources away from football. However, in our case, and in most businesses, execution is not just one more thing—it is the thing. Greatness hinges on execution. Everything we do should ultimately contribute to superior levels of execution."

"Greatness hinges on execution. Where have I heard that before?" Megan asked.

"That's something Jack Deluca taught me years ago."

"As I remember, he also had a lot to say about *how* you lead, didn't he?" Megan asked.

"Yes, he said if leaders aren't careful, we can get sucked into the day-to-day frenetic pace of our lives, and while lost in today's busyness, we can jeopardize our future."

"What did he call this tendency?" Megan paused as if trying to remember.

Blake was onto her little game. "Jack called this reactionary approach to leadership *checkers*. And he challenged me to play chess. Now, are you happy? I said it."

Everything we do should ultimately contribute to superior levels of execution.

"Are you playing chess or checkers when it comes to execution?" she asked.

Blake said nothing.

"Stumped, huh? Okay, here's an easier question: What did Jack say about chess, not checkers?"

"To quote you from earlier in this conversation, 'A lot!'"

"I know. But weren't there some 'moves'?"

"Yes, high performance organizations make four moves: they Bet on Leadership, Act as One, Win the Heart, and Excel at Execution."

"Oh, now I remember," Megan said, pretending to catch up. "What's your next move?"

"I have at least three action items: Talk with Ashley and ask her to create an improvement plan. Thank Paul for his leadership and see how I can help. And go back to my notes from Jack and see what I've missed on the road to Excel at Execution."

A New Day

When Blake called Paul about setting up a meeting, he was delighted to learn Paul already had a breakfast scheduled with a candidate for the new head coach job. As it turned out, Coach Stone was eager to retire when presented with the opportunity. He was tired—forty years of coaching had taken a toll on him. Paul agreed it would be appropriate for Blake to join him and the candidate for the beginning of his interview.

~

Blake had fond memories of breakfasts with his dad at this same local diner. He remembered the long talks, warm pancakes, and chocolate milk. He knew the food would be great and hoped the conversation would be the beginning of a new day for the school.

As he entered the diner, he saw that Paul was already there with a tall, fit man who appeared to be in his midfifties.

"Good morning, Blake. This is Thomas Moore."

"My friends call me Tom," he said.

"Tom, Blake Brown is a local CEO and the chairman of our school board. I wouldn't ordinarily include Blake in an interview, but as a 'get to know you' opportunity, I thought he could join us for some pancakes."

"Fantastic," Tom said. "Great to meet you both. I'm excited to learn more about your story."

Over some amazing food, each man shared milestones and defining moments from his journey. Blake told about his dad's untimely death and his efforts to learn to lead. Paul discussed the tension he managed moving from the classroom as a teacher to become the head of school and the joy he found in his current role. Then it was Tom's turn.

"I've been so fortunate," he began. "I have an amazing wife, Lucy, and three kids: Betty is thirteen, Will is twenty-one, and Jane is twenty-five. I've been coaching my entire life—not literally, but practically." He told about his father, who was also a coach, and growing up in locker rooms as a kid.

"How's your track record as a coach?" Blake asked.

"We've won a few games," Tom said with a wry smile.

Paul said, "I'll take it from here. I don't want to make you blow your own horn. Tom's teams have won fifteen state championships with an overall winning percentage of 84 percent."

"That's impressive!" Blake said. "How long have you been coaching?"

"Almost thirty years, if you don't count the years diagramming plays at the dinner table with my dad," Tom said.

"Were you a player?"

"Yes, I played in college and a little beyond that."

"A little beyond that?" Blake quizzed him.

"Yes, I played a couple of years in the NFL. I was good but couldn't make a career of it," he chuckled. "I'm thankful I had a shot. But I knew all along I would coach. It's what I was born to do."

"Why would you be interested in coming to our school. As I'm sure you know, we don't have a championship pedigree," Blake confessed.

"That's a fair question. First, my dad lives in your area. His health is failing. I want to be near him during his fourth quarter."

"Makes sense."

"But just to be clear, I have no concerns about your past performance."

"Why not?" Paul asked.

"Your past does not determine your future. The absence of championships has no bearing on the future of your program. The fundamentals work regardless of geography, socioeconomic standing, or pedigree."

Blake said, "When you say fundamentals, are you talking about blocking and tackling?"

"Yes, for sure, but the players will learn so much more. There are Fundamentals of Execution that transcend the game of football."

~

For Blake's next executive committee meeting, he asked Ashley to attend and make the presentation she had shared with him the previous week.

"Good morning!" Blake said. "I hope you had a great weekend. I want to introduce you to Ashley Westman. Some of you may have met her already. She's the new head of Production. One of the things you guys know I love about new people is their 'fresh eyes.'

"To capitalize on her unbiased perspective, I asked Ashley to do an audit of our performance. Working with her team, she's done that. Today, she'll share her findings and talk about the way forward. Sandeep, I know Ashley is part of your larger team. Is there anything you want to say before she begins?"

Sandeep, an engineer by training, had been head of Operations for a couple of years. He had mixed emotions about Ashley's report. He knew the data was accurate and her methodology sound, but the report was ultimately an indictment of his team's performance.

"Ashley is going to raise some important questions for us to grapple with. I can promise you her work has been thoughtful and thorough."

"Welcome, Ashley," Blake said. "Why don't you begin by telling everyone a little about your background and then share what you and your team have learned."

Ashley shared a very brief bio and continued, "Thanks, Blake, for allowing me to share a little of my story, but today is not about me. Let's begin with what we learned. As you know, we are an extremely successful company with a solid reputation and healthy margins. Thanks to your leadership, we've attracted great people and built a strong culture. However, during our assessment, we did discover an opportunity."

"I would call it a storm brewing on the horizon," Blake added.

"You guys can decide the threat level. Before I unveil the issue, I want to acknowledge the complexity and scale of our business. Our employees are asked to do literally millions of tasks every day. But behind those tasks, you can find the shadow side of our success: we are not great at the details."

"What does that mean?" asked Kim.

"Well, to avoid subjecting you to hundreds of pages of data, I've created a single slide to represent our level of execution over the last sixty months."

"Execution? Is that what you are calling our 'opportunity?'" Roger Stewart, chief legal counsel, asked.

"Yes. Here's the graph," Ashley said as she projected the image on the screen.

"What is the scale?"

"It is an index based on a one-hundred point scale."

"Okay," Blake jumped in. "What do you see?"

"Our execution was better five years ago," Roger mused.

"Okay, what caused it to fall?" Blake asked.

"I'm guessing increased volume and complexity," Kim speculated.

"What else do you see?"

"It has leveled off. We've been flat for the last two years. Perhaps this is the new normal," Sandeep offered.

"I have a question," Jessica Williams, the CFO, asked. "What's *in* the index? What do these numbers represent?"

"Errors, defects, returns, delays, waste, failure to meet requirements, customer complaints, and more," Ashley said. "I know that may not be helpful, but let me give you a tangible example.

"Order accuracy is part of the calculation—today, we are at 93 percent. Now I don't know how that sounds to you—maybe you're thinking that represents a solid A. If this were algebra, you could be proud. But consider the flip side. Today, for every one hundred orders shipped, seven will be wrong. Good for you if you are one of the lucky ones, but seven out of every hundred will get an incorrect order."

"But we're really good at customer service," Kim said, half joking.

"You are correct—a muscle we've had to strengthen. Our help desk takes thousands of calls a year responding to our poor execution—calls that could be avoided if we did things right. What would happen if our reputation for accuracy and execution rivaled our reputation for customer service? What would happen to our cost structure if we didn't need to devote an entire team to cleanup work? How much stronger could our brand be if we consistently delivered at world-class levels?" Ashley asked.

What would happen if our reputation for accuracy and execution rivaled our reputation for customer service?

Blake jumped back in: "Okay, ladies and gentlemen, we need to decide if our current level of execution is good enough. Ashley and her team will approach the work very differently if we are content with maintaining our current status as opposed to elevating it. Honestly, our decision will also impact our planning and budgeting. We will not drift to greatness. If we go there, it will be because of disciplined and thoughtful actions executed consistently over time."

The first question did not surprise Blake. "What will it cost?" Jessica asked.

"Hard to say," Blake offered. "Here's my question for you guys: What does it cost now to have only 93 percent of our orders shipped correctly?" This sparked a lively debate and some finger-pointing.

Ashley sat quietly as the conversation continued. After a few minutes, Blake interrupted and said, "We're not going to play the blame game—we don't need to. It's my fault. I own this. It happened on my watch. I'm asking you to help me decide what, if anything, we should do to right the ship.

"Now, I want to go back to the cost question—not an insignificant one. And no, I don't think any of us know today what the actual dollar costs will be to fix this problem; we'll figure that out and move with an appropriate pace and rigor. I just want to be sure we're thinking broadly enough about the implications of this issue.

"What does it say about us as a brand to have 7 percent of our customers receive a wrong or incomplete order—today? While we're sitting here!" Blake's energy ticked up just a notch. He remained professional, but his passion for this issue was clearly growing. "If we don't change something, literally millions of our customers will not have a great experience with our brand this year alone. What does that cost over time?

"Now, I've been thinking about this issue a couple of weeks, so I'm probably a little ahead of you. I know you may need to consider more deeply the implications for your area of the business, but what's stopping us from attacking this? Any initial thoughts? Other than the perceived cost."

"We'll probably have to answer a few people questions," Charles said.

"Like what?" Blake asked.

"Do we have the right people for the specific roles? Have they been trained properly? Are they being coached well?"

Kim added, "Do the people even care?"

Based on what Blake knew about engagement, this was not an insignificant question. "That's on us," he added. "Remember what we told people about creating a place where they would feel cared for? We have to deliver on that promise, or we can forget about elite levels of execution."

"At the risk of piling on," Ashley said, "I'm not sure we have the best systems and processes in place today."

"I'm assuming we can fix those," Blake said.

"We can—*if* we want to," Ashley said.

"Are we good enough? That is the question we started with, and we've come full circle. I say we are not," Blake concluded.

The room was quiet, each member of the executive team awkwardly looking at the others. Blake finally said, "I say we at least learn what would be required to go to the next level. Ashley, please put together a proposal and we'll talk again soon."

🏆 Game On!

Paul decided Coach Moore was the best man for the job and made him an offer. After Tom was hired, his first request was to address the entire high school. This was a little odd, since no coach had ever done anything like this before, but obviously, Tom was no ordinary coach.

The assembly was announced and over five hundred kids filed into the gym, not knowing what to expect. All they had been told was they were about to meet a new faculty member. Blake, exercising some of his privilege as a board member, stood in the back of the room, excited to hear what Tom would say.

At the top of the hour, as scheduled, even though some of the kids had not found their seats, the lights went down, and a professionally produced video of the highlights from the past decade of football at the school began to play. The music was loud and the visuals compelling for about ninety seconds, and then the program stopped abruptly—no musical crescendo, no compelling still frame of someone holding a trophy, no fade to black—it just stopped. The lights came on, and Tom took the stage.

"Hi, I'm Tom Moore, your new football coach. Did you like the video?" A few kids nodded and about a dozen clapped.

"Well, like many of you, I had mixed feelings," Tom said. "At least two things were wrong with that video: First, too few of you were in the picture—and not just the players. Did you notice the stands? They were practically empty. Next, and most importantly, that video created a distorted view of winning. It only showed the big plays and the touchdowns. And because of prevailing misconceptions about success, the video crew did all their work on game days. Winning is not confined to game days. The best way to win on game day is to learn how to Win Every Day.

The best way to win on game day is to learn how to Win Every Day.

"Did anyone notice the video wasn't finished? When the editor asked me about the ending, I told her it had not been written yet.

"I'm thankful to be your new coach. Together, we'll write the next chapter of this story, but more importantly, we're going to help some of you write *your* next chapter.

"I want to invite all of you guys to show up for tryouts—even if you have never played football. I promise those of you willing to embrace the challenge will learn, grow, sweat, and win in more ways than you could ever imagine.

"Now, for those not interested in playing but who still want to be part of something great—ladies, you too—there is a place for many of you on this team as well. We need trainers, equipment managers, statisticians, logistics coordinators, communication specialists, camera operators, coaching assistants, and support staff. It will require all of us to make this team successful. If we do this right, we'll have more people supporting the players than we have players," he said with a smile. "Join us and help us create something legendary!

"For those of you who choose not to join the team, we still need your support. We will do our best to represent you and the school well—we want to make you proud.

"Bottom line—I'm inviting *all of you* to join us. If you do, you will learn so much more than how to win on game day. You will learn how to Win Every Day for the rest of your life." Tom turned and left the stage.

Paul was surprised at the brevity of Tom's remarks. He was trying to decide if he should say anything—like maybe tell the kids about his fifteen state championships—but before he could decide what to do, one of the seniors stood and began to clap. In a moment, a few more, and then hundreds of kids were standing and cheering for their new coach and their team and school.

After the assembly, Blake stood alone in the gym, thinking about what he had just witnessed. The students were now full of hope and promise, and once again, Blake was reminded of the power of vision.

Blake wanted to share a similar message with his team, but he didn't feel prepared. His next step was to reach out to Tom to see if he could get some coaching of his own.

～

At dinner, the conversation focused as usual on the day's events. "How was school today?" Megan asked Kristen.

"Good. But there's this guy who won't get over me," she said. "It makes the day a little stressful."

"Do I need to talk to him?" Blake asked.

"Dad, seriously? No. I can talk to him myself."

"I'm sure it'll all work out fine." Megan then turned her attention to Clint. "How about your day, buddy?"

"I'm going to play football."

"What?" Megan said. "Where did this come from? You've never wanted to play before. Do you even know how to play football?"

"Mom—of course I know how to play."

"Why do you need to play with all those big guys?" Megan was scrambling for a good reason her baby boy, now seventeen, shouldn't play football.

"Honey, help me here," she said to Blake.

"I'm not sure I can. I want to play too!" Blake laughed.

"What are you talking about? Have both of you lost your minds?" Megan asked.

"I met the new coach today," Clint said.

"I met him last week, but I heard him speak today too," Blake added.

Megan, confused, said, "Blake, how did you meet him? Why were you at the school? What's going on here?"

"So many questions. Can we take them one at a time?" Blake responded. "Clint, tell your mother what the coach said that makes you want to try out for the team."

Clint replayed the coach's brief remarks almost verbatim.

"Which part of that inspires you?" Megan asked.

"It's hard to say exactly. I have a sense Coach is the real deal. He invited me to try out. But now that I think about it, it was his closing that got me."

"What did he say?" Megan asked.

Clint, looking at Blake, said, "Dad, do you remember?"

"I do, son."

"Tell Mom what Coach said." Clint wanted a coconspirator to help defuse his mom's anxiety.

"He challenged everyone to join him and learn how to win not just on game day—but how to Win Every Day."

Clint jumped back in: "I love that! You guys have challenged me. You've encouraged me. You've funded all sorts of adventures and learning experiences, and you've modeled so many good things for me and Kristen—I just want to keep going, and I think Coach can help me take my next step."

"Blake?" Megan said.

"What do you want me to say? By the way, Tom—Coach Moore—has won fifteen state championships." Blake smiled.

"Really? He didn't mention that," Clint exclaimed. "I knew he was legit."

Megan looked at Blake. "You're not helping here."

"Sorry."

"Clint, you have to promise me you'll be careful." That was all Megan could find to say.

"Yes, ma'am."

Clint gave Blake a high five as he left the table; Megan gave him a look.

~

Under the circumstances of the previous evening, Blake had not mentioned his plan to ask Tom if he would coach him too; however, Blake still made the call.

"I would love to meet with you," Tom said. "How about lunch today?"

"I'll make it happen," Blake said. With a little calendar magic, he arranged to meet with Tom at the diner.

"The breakfast is good, but the burgers are the best," Blake said to Tom.

After the two were seated, Blake said, "Your talk yesterday was really impressive."

"Thank you."

"Man, by the time you finished, I wanted to suit up too."

"You're kind."

"I assume you have given that talk before."

"Versions of it, probably one hundred thousand times."

"Seriously?"

The waitress approached to take their orders. "Burger, fries, and a chocolate shake for me," Blake said.

"I'm just going to follow this guy's lead—I'll have the same," Tom said.

"Hey, before we jump back in, how is your dad?"

"He's doing okay. Thanks for asking. He is thrilled my family has moved to town."

"I bet. Do you have brothers and sisters?"

"No, I'm it. That just added a little pressure to be close by. Again, thanks for asking."

"Back to your talk. You said one hundred thousand times?"

"Yeah, parts, pieces, or versions, although probably more."

"Help me here. How is that possible?"

"Most of the time, I give *myself* that talk. Many times every day."

"Which part?"

"The challenge to Win Every Day," Tom said.

"Yeah, it's a great slogan, but how do you do it—Win Every Day?" Blake asked skeptically.

"It all boils down to our choices. If I don't make the right choices, my team never will. I want to help the team understand this."

If I don't make the right choices, my team never will.

"That sounds like a big idea," Blake said.

"I think so. It's just one in a long list of big ideas my dad taught me."

Tom, attempting to hold his emotions in check, revealed in an instant the fact his dad was probably not doing so well. Brushing away a tear as it rolled down his cheek, he said, "Tell me why you wanted to meet. I mean I really do appreciate the hospitality, but it's not every day a CEO and board chairman invites me to lunch. Am I in trouble already?"

"Sorry, I guess I should explain. Not with me; now my wife, Megan, is another story."

"What's up with Megan?"

"Clint, my seventeen-year-old, came home from school yesterday and announced he's going to try out for your team."

"Oh, and this meeting . . ."

"No, no, no special favor or treatment. As far as you're concerned, he's just another kid. This meeting has nothing to do with that. I only mentioned Clint to let you know you *are* in trouble with my wife. However, I did want this meeting to ask you for a favor."

"Really?"

"Yes, I'm too old and slow to try out for the team, but I would still like to learn from you. What you've done over the course of your career is impressive. I'm not asking for a lifetime commitment, but I would like to know if we can meet from time to time so I can learn some of the lessons your dad shared with you."

"What exactly would we talk about?" Tom was testing Blake to see how much thought he had put into his request.

"My company is really good but not great. We're a lot like the football program you just inherited. Paul's answer was to bring in a new coach. I don't want my board to bring in a new coach—*I am the coach.* I want to fix the problem!"

"What exactly is the problem as you currently see it?"

"That's a good question, one I've been wrestling with," Blake said. "At this point, I'm convinced the biggest problem is me. I have allowed us to get into this situation. So first, it is a leadership issue.

"Second, and more specifically, it appears to be a breakdown in execution. As I think about your world, it could be compared to designing a great play on the whiteboard, but in the game, someone blows their assignment and you lose ten yards."

"Got it. Dad would say, 'Great plays are worthless without great execution.'"

"Exactly. I need you to help me lead at a higher level so I can help my team execute at a higher level."

"Let's agree to meet a few times and reevaluate. If we decide it's a good use of time, we'll continue," Tom suggested.

"Agreed."

Pursue Mastery

A record number of students came out for the first day of tryouts. The coach's talk had signaled he might be different—the next week was about to prove it.

"Okay, guys. Let me tell you about how the tryouts are going to work. The process will take five days and involve some homework." A collective groan arose from the boys.

"We have three fundamentals on this team. We'll invest one afternoon on each. Then, days four and five will include a physical assessment and some drills. You'll run, jump, lift, and run some more. One of our goals is to never play a team in better physical condition than us. If you join the team, physical fitness will become part of your life."

Clint raised his hand. "Yes, Clint, do you have a question?"

"Yes, sir. Two now: how do you know my name?"

Everyone laughed.

"I met you when you came in the room," Coach said.

"But there are a lot of us," Clint said in disbelief.

"Yes."

"Do you know everyone's name?"

"Maybe not everyone's—but I will soon." He smiled. "Was that your second question?"

"Technically, yes, but I do have one more. You mentioned homework. Can you tell us more about that?"

"Sure. At the end of each day, I'll give you an assignment. You'll need to bring it with you the next day.

"Today, let's begin at the beginning. Our first fundamental is Pursue Mastery. What does this mean to you?"

Several hands went up.

"Bob, what do you think?"

"I'm not sure." He paused. "What is mastery?"

"Thanks for asking," Tom said. "Mastery is a level of skill in which three things are true: the desired behavior is consistent, execution is flawless, and the behavior is second nature."

"Does second nature mean it's easy?" John asked.

"No, it won't always be easy to make your block; the guy on the other side of the ball is going to do everything in his power to make it really hard for you.

"However, as you Pursue Mastery, the technique will become second nature. You'll know instinctively through repetition the proper stance, the position of your hands. You'll keep your head up and your back straight. You'll be able to focus on your assignment and your opponent rather than your mechanics."

"Is there a goal associated with this idea of mastery?" Jamal asked.

"Great question. Yes, that's linked to the second attribute I mentioned—to execute flawlessly. Our goal is to do the right thing the right way every time."

"That's scary." One boy said out loud what many were thinking. Several laughed.

Mastery is a level of skill in which three things are true: the desired behavior is consistent, execution is flawless, and the behavior is second nature.

"Don't be intimidated by the goal. It is *not* the expectation—it is the *goal*."

"What's the difference?" someone shouted out.

"They are worlds apart. A goal is something you strive to achieve. An expectation, on the other hand, is, well—expected. When we don't meet a goal, we try again. When we fail to meet expectations, it can cut to our core and over time can create anxiety, frustration, and ultimately resignation. Expectations create pressure, but the right goals inspire and motivate. I don't really like pressure, but I love being motivated," Tom said. "Any other questions?"

Brian raised his hand. "Yes, Brian, what's your question?"

"It's more of a clarification."

"Shoot."

"I'm a lineman. Do you expect me to make my block on every play?"

"No, Brian, I don't."

"Coach, I'm sorry, but that sounds weird."

"Okay, Brian, you've played football for how many years?"

"Eleven years."

"Let me ask you, have you made your block successfully on *every* snap you've ever played?"

"No, sir, I haven't."

"Do you think you'll make every block successfully for the rest of your football career?"

"No, sir, I won't."

"Great, that tells me you are human. Humans are not perfect. If I know you are going to occasionally miss your block, why would I want to put pressure on you to do what you are incapable of doing? Now, back to your question. If you play on this team, your *goal* will be to make your block every time. And we'll work together to help you get better and better so it will be rare when you miss one. So, the essence of Pursue Mastery is the decision and the resulting personal effort to do whatever you are doing right. It is a lifelong pursuit.

"Okay, this has been a really good conversation. I want you to get in groups of three or four and spend the next few minutes talking about some of the things you'll need to do if you choose to Pursue Mastery. What are some real-world, practical implications of our first fundamental?"

The boys organized themselves in groups and began discussing the question. After a few minutes, the coach stopped the discussion.

"Let's hear a few of your answers. No need to raise your hands—just shout it out."

"Memorize the plays."

"Listen to the coaches."

"I like that one," Tom laughed. "Other ideas?"

"Get enough rest."

"Stay in good physical shape."

"A few more?" Tom said. "Logan, do you have something to add?"

"When faced with a choice, you have to decide in the moment which option will lead to mastery. I'm pretty sure not all paths will get you there."

"Okay, let's talk about that for a moment. What are some dead ends we want to avoid?" Tom asked.

This question created a buzz among the players. "Shout out your answers," Tom encouraged.

"Shortcuts."

"Cheating."

"Performance-enhancing drugs."

"You are all correct. Anything else?"

Clint said, "Half-hearted effort. I'm guessing the pursuit of mastery means going all in."

"Exactly. Here's something else. Pursue Mastery is not a one-time decision. If you choose this path, you will constantly be confronted with opportunities to take a step toward or away from mastery. The way of mastery will require countless daily decisions—on and off the field and long after you graduate from this school."

The boys shared many other ideas, some very personal, as the challenge implied in Pursue Mastery began to sink in. With every comment, they gained more and more clarity regarding what would be required. The first fundamental was no joke!

"Any final thought? Who wants the last word?" Tom asked.

Boyd raised his hand.

"Yes, Boyd."

"I'm going to have to quit whining and making excuses."

"Thanks for your honesty," Tom said. "What you just said is true for me too. If I am not very careful, I can blame others and think of a dozen reasons I didn't do the right thing the right way. However, my choices are mine and mine alone. This realization has made a profound difference in my coaching—and my life. This first fundamental has literally changed my life. If you choose to Pursue Mastery, it will change your life too.

If I am not very careful, I can blame others and think of a dozen reasons I didn't do the right thing the right way.

"Thanks for your energy and engagement today! Here's your homework: write a summary of what we discussed today and bring it with you tomorrow. We're almost done here. Hit the track and run one mile before you leave. For you new guys, that's four *full* laps."

~

When Clint went home, he could hardly wait to tell his dad about the first day of tryouts.

As they sat discussing the day, Blake was mesmerized. He and Clint both recognized this was not a tryout as much as an extended orientation. The coach was trying to determine who would embrace his fundamentals *before* they ever took the field.

When Clint went to his room to write his summary, Blake sat considering the implications for his organization. He decided to talk with Ashley about their Fundamentals of Execution—he was fairly sure they didn't have any.

~

The next morning, Blake was up early. He made his way to the office and sent Ashley a text: "Love to meet today if you have a few minutes."

A short while later, Ashley was sitting in Blake's office.

"Thanks for making time to meet, Ashley. I will try to give you more notice in the future. I just had a few updates I wanted to share with you. How is your plan coming along to help us improve our execution?" Blake asked.

"We're making progress. Should have some preliminary ideas to you soon."

"Good. I want to tell you about a little research I'm doing on my own." Blake proceeded to tell Ashley about the new coach, his winning percentage, and his unorthodox approach to tryouts.

"I'm not assuming his methods will work for us, but I think this could be an interesting case study."

"Agreed. What have you learned so far?" Ashley asked.

"The coach has three Fundamentals of Execution, and the first one is Pursue Mastery."

"Interesting. What else can you tell me?"

"Not much, but here's how I would summarize what I do know: Tom believes no individual, team, or organization will ever drift to greatness. The journey always begins with a conscious choice."

"I agree," Ashley said.

"I knew you would. You have been very consistent with your question, 'Are we good enough?' In essence, you are asking us if we are going to Pursue Mastery or not.

"What would we have to do to Pursue Mastery?" Blake asked as if thinking out loud, not expecting a response.

"We would have to define it first," Ashley said.

"Coach has a definition: he wants the desired behaviors to be consistent, flawless, and second nature."

"Flawless sounds like an unrealistic expectation," she responded.

"Yeah, Tom would agree. That's why he says their *goal* is to do the right thing the right way every time. It's the goal, *not the expectation*. Coach says expectations, specifically the really lofty ones, can demotivate, but big goals inspire."

"That helps," Ashley said.

"What else would we have to do?"

"Lots of vision casting from you and other leaders would be necessary."

"Why do you say that?"

"I'm afraid the goal around here is *not* 'do the right thing the right way every time.' It's probably closer to 'good enough is good enough.'"

"Ouch!" Blake said.

"Painful, I know. That's why you'll have to help people understand the why behind our efforts. Change is hard—even harder if people don't know why you're trying to change. You and other leaders will need to paint a compelling picture of the future, help people see the value inherent in pursuing mastery. If people aren't convinced, they just won't do it."

Blake nodded in agreement, "Tom knows winning every day begins with an individual, and very personal, decision. That's why Pursue Mastery is the first fundamental."

Own the Numbers

The next afternoon, Coach was in the hallway greeting players and collecting their homework. Everything was going well until Daryl showed up without his assignment.

"I'm sorry, Daryl, you'll not be able to join the team."

"Why not?"

"You don't have your homework."

"I was busy."

"I'm sure you were."

"Are you kidding me?"

"No. Unfortunately, I am not. I'm sorry." The guys who heard the exchange were stunned. This coach was for real! Tragically, or maybe not, five other guys didn't do the assignment either. They were all dismissed. The coach said nothing to the entire group about what had happened. At the top of the hour, he began.

"Thanks for coming back and for doing your homework. I look forward to reading every one of your summaries. They will not be graded," he said, smiling, "but here's what I will do: if, based on your work, it appears I have not communicated clearly, I'll talk with you individually to clarify my intent. Also, I'll share some of your responses with the team in the days and weeks ahead.

"Today, we're going to talk about our second fundamental—actually, you are going to experience it. Let's head to the bus. You can leave your bag in your locker." After a short ride, the team arrived at the local bowling alley. The coach addressed the team before they got off the bus.

"Okay, we're going bowling this afternoon," Tom said. The boys cheered.

"When you get off the bus, you'll be given your lane assignment; your shoes will be waiting at your lane."

As Clint and the others made their way to their lanes, they noticed something different about this bowling alley. The end of each lane had been draped with a heavy cloth concealing the pins—only a small space remained at the bottom to allow the ball to go under the fabric. As the boys found their lanes and balls, most of them stood gawking at the situation.

Coach, speaking through the PA system, said, "You can start bowling now."

Though the setting was strange and bordering on the bizarre, each boy rolled his ball toward the uncertain target. If he didn't roll a gutter ball, everyone could hear the pins falling, but no one knew how many fell.

Joe rolled the ball and said, "I think I got a strike!"

Jamal, his lane partner, said, "I think you got about five."

The boys lost interest quickly. Tom noticed and addressed the group, "Guys, you are supposed to be bowling. Some of you have asked how you're doing. Just keep rolling the ball and try to get better."

After about thirty minutes, the coach was about to have a mutiny on his hands. He addressed the group a third time. "How's it going?"

"We don't know," someone yelled.

"What do you mean you don't know?" Tom asked.

"We can't see the pins. Can we stop now?" Kyle exclaimed.

"Okay, I'll give you a ten-minute break. The snack bar is open."

After the boys left their lanes, the staff quickly removed the drapes that had been covering the pins. When the boys returned from the break, they had an almost immediate boost in energy when they realized they could now see the pins!

The coach said, "Okay, you can continue bowling."

The boys' engagement changed instantly. They were keeping score, talking trash, competing, and even celebrating with each other. After the first game was completed, the coach called the boys together.

They were genuinely reluctant to stop what an hour earlier had been drudgery.

"Let's talk about what just happened here," the coach said.

"The first half hour sucked," Kyle said. Everyone laughed.

"Why?"

"Coach, you know why. We couldn't see the pins!" Jesse said.

"Why does that matter? The activity in both rounds was the same: all you were asked to do was roll the ball down the lane and try to improve."

"If we couldn't see the pins, we couldn't improve."

"Anything else?"

"We couldn't keep score either," Clint said.

"What else was different in round two, other than seeing the pins?" the coach asked.

"It was more fun," Cameron said.

"We cheered for each other."

"And talked some smack."

"We improved too."

"So, if you had a choice, would you rather participate in round one or round two?" Tom asked.

Almost in unison the boys shouted, "Round two."

"Our second fundamental is Own the Numbers.

"We're going to create an environment in which you will always know the numbers. But as you can guess, knowing the numbers won't be enough. You will have to own them, personally."

A hand went up.

"Yes, Franco."

"What numbers are we supposed to own? I mean here, it seems easy—how many pins we knock down. I think owning the numbers will be harder for us in football."

Kyle added, "Yeah, we all play different positions."

Chris jumped in: "But what if everyone knew the overall numbers—like the score? I think we would play differently. That's what happened here today. We played *very* differently when we knew the score. I tried harder when I could see the pins." There seemed to be general agreement with Chris's statement. "When we weren't keeping score, I really didn't care," he said.

"All three of you are right! It will be a little more challenging for us because of the different roles, *and* there is still value in everyone knowing the overall score. Regarding your question, Franco, you will have role-specific numbers and team numbers. That's one of our responsibilities as coaches—to help you know the numbers. Then you can own them."

"Coach, I'm trying to figure out what it means to 'own' a number," Franco said.

"What do you guys think?" Coach asked the group. The ideas came quickly.

"To really care about the number."

"To work to improve it."

"To accept responsibility for the number."

"Darnell, do you have a thought?"

"No, I was just stretching," he said, triggering muffled laughter around the room.

"Anyone else?" Coach asked.

Kyle was next: "I still need some help here. Bowling is one thing. What kind of numbers are you thinking about for us?"

Coach said, "Any suggestions?" No one spoke up.

Luis said, "I think the reason people are quiet is the answer seems kinda obvious."

"Good. What is the obvious answer?" Tom asked.

"Wins," Luis said.

"Good guess, but that's not what I am suggesting. Wins are the outcome of a lot of hard work, but they are not where we'll place our focus. We want to measure activities that will help us win more games. Which numbers do you think would be helpful?" Tom asked.

"Yards per carry?"

"Sure. What else?"

"Points allowed."

"True. Others?" The room was still.

"How about how many of your blocks or tackles you make successfully or routes the receivers run correctly? How about your personal best in the weight room? Or the number of hours of sleep you get every night? The answer to all of these is yes," the coach said. "We will track specific activities and behaviors that help us improve our performance."

"As you can imagine, there are many appropriate numbers we can own, and you can begin to see why this is a fundamental we must embrace if we want to Win Every Day. Any other thoughts or questions?"

"I have one," Clint said. "I think we can set better goals."

"You are correct. Do you have an example?"

"Not really," Clint said.

We want to measure activities that will help us win more games.

Tom said, "Let me give you one. If you play on the offensive line, we will evaluate every snap. You will know how you performed this week versus last week. As Clint suggested, it is much easier to set improvement goals when you have real data. 'I want to play better' is a great aspiration but a lousy goal."

Tim, a senior on the team, said, "If we are measuring stuff, we can also hold each other accountable."

"Thanks, Tim. What could that look like?"

"I'm not really sure, but if we measure who comes late to practice, we can call out guys who are late."

"Okay, I follow your logic and agree with the concept. However, we will not need to measure late to practice."

"Why not?"

"Because no one is going to be late to practice," Tom said with a big smile. "I want to say one more thing about this idea of accountability. Tim, thanks for bringing this up. You are correct, if we Own the Numbers, we can hold each other accountable, but more importantly, we can hold *ourselves* accountable."

If we Own the Numbers, we can hold each other accountable, but more importantly, we can hold *ourselves* accountable.

"What does that look like?" Ivan asked.

"We will be tracking the number of hours we sleep each night; you will keep your own records. You will be accountable to the team, for sure, but your first accountability is to yourself. You will Own the Numbers. If you choose to Pursue Mastery, you will do what that decision demands, and personal accountability will become a way of life. Here's the bottom line: When we measure what matters and Own the Numbers, our results will improve."

"Now, for your homework. For those who have played football before, come up with three potential activities or outcomes you could measure based on the last position you played. If you played multiple positions, choose your favorite. After you've identified your three metrics, tell me why these would be helpful.

"For those of you new to the game, pick a position you would like to play. If you need some help, you can talk with one of the coaches after practice or you can Google it," Tom said smiling. "You need to come up with three things you could measure as well and why they would matter to you and the team."

~

Once again, Clint's plan was to share the day's events with his dad after dinner. Blake was excited to learn the second fundamental. He couldn't believe the team did "blind bowling." "Genius," he said.

"What position are you going to try out for?" Blake asked.

"I've been giving that a lot of thought," Clint said. "Probably going to say kicker or punter."

"Have you ever kicked or punted a football?"

"Nope, but ten years of soccer can't hurt my chances," he chuckled.

"Good thinking."

~

The next morning during breakfast, Clint came down the stairs about an hour early with a little more energy than usual.

"What's up, buddy? You're up early," Megan said.

"Yeah, I'm meeting Kyle this morning before school. He's the kicker on our team. I want to ask him to be my mentor."

"Tell me more," Megan said.

"Dad, can you fill Mom in? I really don't want to be late."

"Sure. One question first."

"Shoot," Clint said, standing by the door, backpack in hand.

"What metrics did you choose?"

"Distance, hang time, and punts out of bounds inside the ten-yard line."

"Fantastic," Blake said.

"Love you guys!" Clint said over his shoulder as he scampered out of the house.

"Okay, fill me in," Megan said.

Blake told her about Clint's homework and his decision to try out for a kicking spot on the team. Megan knew football well enough to know Clint's choice made sense, and from a mother's point of view, she was relieved—it was probably the safest position on the field.

🏆 Reality Check

Blake was eager to talk with Ashley again. However, she was out of town attending a conference, so he decided to do some independent research. He wanted to assess the company's current reality as it related to Tom's second fundamental. He would use the time between his meetings to visit with some of the employees on various teams. First stop: Customer Service.

"Good morning, Suzy," Blake said.

"To what do we owe this unexpected visit?" Suzy asked.

"I'm just trying to stay in touch," Blake said with a smile.

"Well, we're in touch," she said.

"I know you are. That's why you were my first stop this morning. How are the numbers this month?"

"Which numbers?" Suzy asked.

"*Your* numbers," Blake said.

"Hmm . . . my numbers. I have four days of vacation left I need to take before the end of the year, and I'm three years and four months from retirement. Is that what you are looking for?"

"That's good to hear. Congratulations on the upcoming retirement, I guess. How's the work going?"

"Really good, I think. I assume no news is good news."

"Any idea how many orders you process in a day or how many returns you handle in a week?"

"A lot! My inbox is full every morning."

"How about your goals?"

"Other than vacation and retirement," she laughed, "I have only one goal."

"And that is?" Blake asked.

"To have an empty inbox by the end of the day."

"Got it."

~

After lunch, Blake headed to Production. He knew this area had some issues based on Ashley's data on execution. He understood that all the errors were not attributable to this group—some issues were shipping and administrative missteps—but the majority of the problems appeared to have their roots in this area. Blake had called ahead and told Joe, Ashley's director of operations, he would be coming by.

"Hi, Blake. Welcome to Production. Sorry Ashley's not here, but you already know that. How can we help you today?"

"I want to talk with you about measurement, and I want to talk with some of your team as well."

"No problem. Where would you like to start?"

"Let's you and I talk for a few minutes first."

"Sounds good."

"But first, how are things going outside of work?" Blake began.

"Outside of work?"

"Yeah, how are Sandra and the kids?"

Joe was a bit surprised Blake remembered Sandra. He knew they met at last year's picnic. "They are doing fine. Little Joe has started school."

"How about Emma—is she still dancing?"

"Why yes, yes, she is. Probably won't make a living at it, but for a middle schooler, she is really good. And with you?" Joe asked.

"Clint has decided to try out for football, and Kristen is just a few years ahead of Emma—starting to think about boys." Blake rolled his eyes.

"I don't look forward to that."

"How are things here at work?" Blake asked.

"Good, I think."

"You think?"

"Well, the orders keep coming, and we continue to produce more and more product. I think that's good."

"It certainly is. How about quality? Ashley tells me we are stagnant on some of our execution numbers."

"Yes, we are. But that's not been our focus."

"What is our focus?"

"Speed. If we don't produce, we don't eat," Joe said smiling.

"There is some truth in that statement. What about errors and defects?"

"We don't like them." Joe smiled again.

"Neither do our customers," Blake confirmed.

"I know. I continue to ask our folks to try harder. They seem to appreciate the encouragement."

"Any key process metrics we can watch to head off mistakes?"

"Maybe. As I said, that's not our focus."

"Yes, I know—speed."

"You got it."

"Thanks for your time today. Can I talk with a few team members on the floor?"

"Sure. Keep in mind they are really busy."

"I know. Just a few questions."

"Let's go."

Blake talked to three team members in different areas of the process. One was new and two, more seasoned. Their stories were strikingly consistent. They weren't measuring anything; they were just attempting to execute their assigned tasks. The other thing they all agreed on: they were supposed to work "faster," although none of them knew what that really meant or if they were making any progress. They were blind bowling—being told every day to roll the ball, faster and faster, with no idea how they were doing.

They were blind bowling— being told every day to roll the ball, faster and faster, with no idea how they were doing.

"Thanks, Joe. This has been very helpful. Please tell Sandra I said hi."

~

Blake really didn't want to jump to any conclusions, but if his first two visits were any indication, Tom's second fundamental was not part of his company's culture.

Blake was "0 for 2" at this point with one visit to go. He was headed to Shipping.

"Hello, Blake!" said a woman with a big voice and an even bigger smile. Gertrude was the head of Shipping and a longtime employee. She had been with the company since its founding, a decade before Blake was named CEO.

"How are you?" Blake said.

"Better than I deserve."

"Me too," Blake acknowledged. "How are things in your world?"

"Tremendous! The children are on their own, and Fred and I are enjoying being empty nesters. Things at work are really good too. How can I help you today?"

"I'm trying to learn more about measurement. How are we tracking our progress here in your area?"

"It's extremely simple: cases shipped. That's our business, and business is good."

"Anything else?"

"What else is there?"

"Any cost metrics?"

"Not really."

"Productivity?"

"No."

"Returns, errors, omissions?"

"No, we let the admin staff sort all that out. We ship," Gertrude said with confidence.

"I see." Blake's mind was racing.

"Any other questions for me?" Gertrude asked. "If not . . ."

"I know, you need to ship!"

"Yes, sir!"

"No, I'm good for now. Please tell Fred I said hello."

Help Others Win

On day three of the tryouts, everyone was in the bleachers before 4:00 p.m. The coach greeted the guys as they came in, but most of them were distracted by the large wooden wall in the center of the gym floor. The almost twelve-foot-high by fifteen-feet-wide wall had no ropes, steps, ladders, or holds.

At the top of the hour, the coach said, "Good afternoon! Your challenge is to get *everyone* over the wall. You have thirty minutes—*go!*"

The group sat there for a moment, not sure exactly what to do next. Then, as if on cue, all the boys jumped to their feet and ran over to see the opponent up close. Close to fifty boys were staring at this wooden beast, and at least as many conversations started almost simultaneously. The kids were buzzing with ideas. The problem was, you couldn't hear any of them. A couple of kids started to climb—or at least attempted to climb, one boosting another, trying to reach the top.

Finally, Brian, a senior, decided to lead.

"Quiet!" he screamed at the top of his lungs.

The group responded with their attention.

"Okay, who has an idea of how we can do this?" With that question, ten guys started talking.

"Hold on," Brian yelled. "One at a time."

The first idea was to throw a little guy up to the top and let him begin a human chain. The group quickly ruled that out. The next was to create smaller teams to work on various solutions the group could test. This was deemed too time consuming. Then, Kyle suggested forming a human pyramid so the guys could climb up and over.

That seemed like a reasonable idea, and Brian called all the big guys to create the base and build from there.

When the pyramid was almost complete, Clint went to Brian and asked a question: "Brian, I can see how this is going to get some of the guys over the top, but how is it going to get everyone over the wall?"

"What do you mean?" Brian asked.

"If we do this as planned, who is going to help the big guys over?"

"You've got a point," he said. "Stop! We need to modify the plan."

A lot of grumbling could be heard, and a few said they wanted to climb over.

"Remember, the goal is to get *everyone* over the wall," he said.

"So—what's your point? We were about to start when you yelled stop."

"Let's think through this. If we do what we've planned, who will help the big guys over the top? Any ideas?"

Brody said, "Yeah, let's help the big guys over first. Maybe they can even pull some guys up from the other side. Then, we'll let the smaller guys with the good verticals go last. All they will need is someone to reach over, grab their hand, and pull them up."

"So, we build the pyramid on this side first and then we build one on the other side too?" Brain asked.

"I think so."

"Let's try it."

The next ten minutes were intense: trying to decide how to get several 250-pound guys over the wall was no easy task. After several failed attempts, they finally got the first guy, Jacob, to the top. He looked like a turtle on a fence post.

Jacob was terrified. "What do I do now?"

The coach called for a few spotters to go to the other side in case Jacob needed any help.

"What's next?" Brian said, looking at Clint, who shrugged his shoulders.

Mike, sensing Brian's uncertainty, jumped in. "Okay, grab the top of the wall and begin to slide down the side just like you were sliding out of bed. How tall are you?"

"What? You want to know how tall I am?"

"Yes."

"I'm six foot six."

"Great. Add that to the length of your arms and once you extend them, you'll only have to drop a few feet to reach the floor."

"Seriously?"

"Yep, that's the plan. Now, slide down the wall."

"And don't forget to hold on," Andy added.

"I can promise you I won't forget," Jacob said.

In a moment, Jacob was standing on the floor on the other side. The team erupted in cheers, hugs, and high fives.

"Okay, focus, guys. We have a lot more guys to go. How are we doing on time?" Kyle asked.

John, the official timekeeper, said, "We have eighteen minutes."

"Okay? Who's the next big guy?" Brian asked.

Clint added, "The tallest of the big guys."

Ben stepped up.

"You know the drill, and Jacob can help you on the other side."

In just a moment, he was on the other side with Jacob.

"Next, who's next? Go ahead and make a line, biggest to smallest. Let's go!"

This direction proved extremely helpful as the guys repeated the moves demonstrated by Jacob and Ben. The majority of the guys required just seconds each to scale the wall. At the same time, the boys on the other side built their own pyramid to help guys down the back of the wall. With ninety seconds left, just two guys remained—Tim and Clint. Tim would provide a boost for Clint, who would grab the extended hand and be pulled to the top. Just as they were about to execute this step in the plan, Tim yelled, "Wait!"

"What? We're about out of time. Give me a boost," Clint said.

"Swap with me—now!" Tim demanded.

"Are you crazy? Don't change the plan now; we're going to lose."

Convinced by the look on Tim's face that he wasn't going to budge, Clint muttered a reluctant "Okay." The two swapped and because Tim was small, he was up and over in a snap. Now with twenty seconds to go, Clint would have to run, jump, and catch the outstretched arm of Jamal, who was extended as far down the wall as he could reach. This strategy meant Clint would have to grab hold of Jamal's hand about nine feet above the ground. Did he have that much lift in his legs? Did Jamal have enough strength to pull him over the top? Could they do all of this in the seconds that remained?

Clint knew he had time for only one leap. He stepped back about twenty feet and stared at the wall, visualizing his jump.

John yelled, "Go, man, go. We only have ten seconds left."

Clint sprinted and burst into the air, grabbing Jamal's arm the way trapeze artists do, and Jamal pulled him over the top. The pile of guys on the other side erupted as the clock ran down to zero. The celebration that followed was pure bedlam. After the high fives, hugs, hoots, and hollers subsided, Tom addressed the team.

"Congratulations, guys! That was impressive. I've been doing that drill with teams for many years, and you are the first to accomplish the goal on the first attempt. Take a seat and let's talk about it. Who wants to describe what happened?"

Kyle, who had not previously said much during tryouts, started: "We did it together."

"Yeah, but why did you do it together?" Tom asked.

"We couldn't be successful without everyone," Clint said.

"Correct. And we really can't Win Every Day without everyone. What else happened?"

We really can't Win Every Day without everyone.

"In the beginning," Chris said, "say, for about the first five minutes, we didn't have a plan."

"We didn't have a leader either," Raj said. "If Brian hadn't stepped up, we wouldn't have had a chance."

"I appreciate that, but here's the truth," Brian added. "The first plan we had wasn't going to work.

Clint recognized that and came to me. That's when I said 'big guys first.' We called an audible based on new information."

"Good, anything else?" Tom asked.

"We physically helped each other do what we couldn't do alone. It's kind of like helping a guy make a critical block," Ruben added.

"You guys also helped me emotionally," Jacob said. "I am *really* scared of heights—when I was on top of the wall, I thought I was going to die. Mike encouraged me. Just knowing you guys were there, and the fact that the coach put some spotters on the back side, really helped me a lot."

"Encouragement is a powerful thing," Tom affirmed. "We're all going to find ourselves on top of a wall at some point. We will need each other to get through it.

"Anything else?" Tom asked. No one appeared to have anything to say. "No? Then I have one more question: did you challenge each other?"

"Not really. We just did what Brian told us to do," Luis said.

"Well, I'm not sure that's accurate," Brian added. "Although Clint is soft-spoken, he was really challenging me when he questioned our plan."

"Tim wasn't soft-spoken when he challenged me," Clint said.

"Tim, tell us what was going on in your head in the moment," Tom asked.

"It was simple. I realized I probably couldn't reach Jamal's hand. Clint is about six inches taller than me. I wasn't sure he could reach it either, but with thirty seconds to go, we didn't have time to debate it. I made the call—he was our best last chance at success, not me."

"That was an outstanding challenge," Tom said. "I wondered if you were going to make the adjustment or not.

"Okay, are you ready for the third and final fundamental? If we are going to Win Every Day, we must Pursue Mastery, Own the Numbers, and Help Others Win. You did this today, and you'll need to do it every day if we are going to reach our full potential. What does it mean to Help Others Win? Shout it out."

"Encourage."

"Lead."

"Challenge."

"Plan."

"Train."

"Listen."

"Anything else?" Tom asked.

"Celebrate," Ben added.

"Absolutely," Tom affirmed. "Let's never miss the chance to celebrate.

"Over the course of the season, we'll learn more ways to Help Others Win. The most important part of this fundamental is for each of you to acknowledge the fact that we cannot Win Every Day without each other; just like we couldn't have gotten over the wall as individuals—you did it together. You still have to make your individual contributions for sure, but the better we are at helping others win, the better we will be as a team."

∼

Clint was exhausted when he got home. He didn't realize how much energy he had just expended. He made his way to his room and collapsed on the bed. He fell into a deep sleep.

An hour later, Megan came knocking. "Honey, want some dinner?"

"Sure, Mom. I'll be down shortly."

When he got downstairs, he found his mom and Kristen at the table. "Where's Dad?"

"He's coming; his meeting ran late. How was day three?"

"Really good. I want to tell you and Dad all about it. Can we talk about it after he gets home?"

"Sure."

The meal was good, the conversation easy, as the family caught up on school, boys, and plans for an upcoming family trip. A few minutes later Blake walked in.

"Good to have you home!" Megan greeted Blake with a kiss. "I have a plate in the oven for you. Clint wants to tell us about his day, but he wanted to wait until you got home."

"I'm ready. Just let me wash up."

When Blake returned to the table, Kristen decided to stay and hear Clint's story.

"Thanks for waiting on me to share about your day. How was it?" Blake asked.

"Amazing! We learned about the third fundamental. But in this case, just like Own the Numbers, Coach didn't tell us, he let us experience it." Clint replayed the entire event in great detail.

"That sounds fun," Kristen said.

"It was," Clint said.

"What is the third fundamental?" Blake asked.

"Help Others Win," Clint said. "We experienced about a dozen different ways we can Help Others Win during that half hour. It was intense."

"What's your biggest takeaway?"

"At the end of the session, Coach said our ultimate success as a team will largely be determined by two factors: individual contribution *and* how well we learn to Help Others Win.

"He said our individual decision to Pursue Mastery and Own the Numbers is foundational, but until we commit to Help Others Win, our success will always be limited. He said over the long haul, a culture of 'we' always outperforms a culture of 'me.'"

"That's the power of the team at its best," Blake said as he drifted into his own thoughts. *Could this third fundamental be the missing ingredient in creating the culture I so desperately want?*

"Dad, hello. . . . Are you with us?"

"Yeah, sorry. I was processing this idea of Help Others Win. It feels big. Once a team or organization embraces this—when 'we' overtakes 'me' in the collective psyche—that's the moment an entirely new culture is born."

Megan said, "I think I'm with you. When everyone in the organization embraces their responsibility to Help Others Win, the ethos of the organization shifts—it becomes a totally different place."

"Yeah, that's what I was pondering when you lost me," Blake admitted. "I need to think about how to make this fundamental part of our culture at work. Clint, what's next?"

"Tomorrow is physical assessment day."

Kristen said, "That doesn't sound like fun."

Ready, Set, Go!

The first three days of the tryouts had been really thought-provoking, but the boys knew today would be different. They were told to meet on the field with their shoulder pads and helmets. The coach and his eight assistants had set up what looked like a mini NFL combine with six stations.

"Good afternoon! Welcome to day four. Today, we are going to assess your fitness level. Now, I have said several things this week about the high level of fitness required to be part of this team. I want all of you to rest easy. Those lofty levels are not required today. Our job is to help you get stronger and faster—today is the baseline. Let's begin with some warm-up drills. Line up on the ten, twenty, thirty, forty, and fifty yard lines, ten players per line."

Mass confusion ensued as the boys tried to figure out their arrangement the first time. The assistant coaches ended up putting several boys in the right position.

"Okay, take a look at where you are on the field and who is standing around you. The next time we say 'Warm-up,' it should take you only about twenty seconds to get in this same formation. One more thing, boys—we run, not walk, when we are on the field."

The team did about fifteen minutes of serious exercise. For some of the guys, this was the most strenuous workout they had ever experienced.

"Next, we're going to run a little," Coach said. "We'll begin with a mile—pace yourselves accordingly. Everyone to the track. For those who don't know, or who have forgotten, we're doing four laps. Ready, set, go!"

The next few minutes told the coaching staff a lot about the challenge before them. A couple of players completed the mile with impressive times—under six minutes. A larger group finished in almost double that, and the balance walked across the finish line; Jacob was the last at just over twenty minutes.

Next, the guys were put in six groups, each assigned to a station manned by a coach. The assessments would cover the 40-yard dash, vertical jump, broad jump, bench press, an obstacle course, and an agility test. When the horn blew, they would rotate to the next station. In an hour, it was over—almost.

"Okay, good job, guys. Time for cooldown. To the track." Some boys jogged. Others began to walk. "We don't walk on the field; we run," Coach bellowed.

The boys quickly regained their composure and ran to the track.

"One mile and you can head to the showers—and no one leaves the field until everyone is finished. Ready, set, go!" Tom said.

The boys moved in a slow wave around the track. After a few of the boys finished, they went back to cheer on the others. When everyone was done except Jacob, Brian and Clint went out to meet him and physically help him across the finish line. All the boys cheered.

"Great day, guys. Here's your homework: send me an email with the names of two guys you'd like to have as your captains. Hit the showers!"

The boys *ran* off the field together; even Jacob was able to lumber to the locker room. The coach knew this was a very good sign.

∿

At home, Clint told his mom about the day. When Blake returned home, he heard the whole story.

"Sounds intense."

"It was, but it was a blast," Clint said.

"Why do you think it was fun?"

"I guess because we did it together. Don't get me wrong; it was hard—but a good hard. Do you know what I mean?"

"I do. What's next?"

"Tomorrow is the last day of tryouts. I think we're going to be with the position coaches. What's next for you, Dad?" Clint asked. "I know you've been thinking hard about how all of this applies to your business."

"I have, and thanks for allowing me to pick your brain. I really do think Tom has some big ideas about what it takes to Win Every Day," Blake said. "To answer your question, I'm still not sure. I have a meeting with Ashley on Monday."

Clint thought day five of tryouts was really cool—the first day that felt like football to him. He and several other guys met with Jake, the special teams coach, who would be responsible for kickoffs—both kicking and receiving—punts, extra points, and field goals. The group meeting with Jake was small in number since most of the guys who staffed these squads also played offensive and defensive positions. For the kickers, Jake watched each player kick and offered on-the-spot coaching. No surprise, he seemed to be fixated on the concept of mastery. "Consistent, flawless, and second nature," he said as he instructed Clint to kick again.

After about ninety minutes of drills, coaching, demonstrations, and affirmations, Jake blew the whistle and the boys ran, not walked, to the fifty-yard line. There Tom addressed the team.

"Boys, thanks for a great week! I am really encouraged by your focus, intensity, and engagement. I want to wind up our tryout with a review of the commitment each of you will have to make if you want to join this team.

"We do not want to win just on game day. In fact, I think that is impossible. To win consistently requires a different mindset. We will win on game day because we Win Every Day. Let me remind you how we are going to do this.

"You must commit to the three fundamentals we discussed earlier this week.

"First, you must make a personal decision to Pursue Mastery—I can't do this for you, your mother can't, and neither can your best friend. We can encourage you and even challenge you, but if you want to be great, you will have to decide. We cannot be as good as we want to be unless you, Brian, and you, Raj, and Ben, and Clint, and every one of you decides in your heart to Pursue Mastery.

We can encourage you and even challenge you, but if you want to be great, you will have to decide.

"Next, if you want to be on this team, you will have to Own the Numbers. We will help you create a scorecard, but you have to own it—care about the numbers, work to improve them, and celebrate with the team when we move them. Again, this is your work. The coaches will do all we can to set you up for success, but until you take personal ownership of the numbers, the team and, more importantly, you will never reach your full potential.

"And finally, this is a team. If you cannot wholeheartedly embrace our third fundamental, Help Others Win, you should not come back. This fundamental is the one that turbocharges our efforts. The support you provide for each other will ultimately set us apart—the encouragement, challenge, and accountability will make us unstoppable. We cannot win without each other.

"A final word about my motivation—if you think this is all about football, you are mistaken. I care about each one of you as a human being, and I want you to Win Every Day for the rest of your life. My plan is for your time on this team to serve as a launching pad for you to accomplish more in your life than you ever imagined possible . . . and, we're going to win a lot of football games! Huddle up."

The boys gathered tightly around the coach, "'Win Every Day' on three," he said in his booming voice. "One two, three."

"Win Every Day!" the entire team shouted in unison.

Coach Jake blew his whistle and said, "Men, run two miles and hit the showers!"

There was no grumbling or moaning, only silent resolve as the team ran toward the track. This time, none of the boys sprinted ahead; they paced themselves with Jacob. They started together and they finished together. This may have been the moment they became a team.

~

When Clint got home, his mom greeted him at the door. "Did you make the team?" Megan asked.

"Um, I don't know. I guess so. Coach never mentioned our next steps. I'll text some of the other guys to see if they know what's happening."

"Do you have big plans tomorrow?"

"I think I'm going to sleep late, and then I need to go for a run."

"Really? Since when are you a runner?"

"Since I learned the coach wants us *all* to be runners," Clint said, smiling.

~

The next morning, Clint had planned to sleep in, but his phone rang at 7:05 a.m.

"Hello," he mumbled, unable to hide his sleep-induced stupor.

"Hey, man, it's Jacob."

"What are you doing up so early on a Saturday morning?"

"The coach just came by."

"He did? Why? What did he say? Why are you calling me?"

"He said I made the team! He gave me a jersey with my name on it! I wanted to thank you."

"Why are you thanking me?"

"I wouldn't have finished that last mile if you hadn't helped me on day four. I just needed to say thanks!"

"Okay, man. Congratulations. I'll see you Monday."

"Hey, do you want to run today?"

"You want to run? Seriously?"

"I need to. Don't you think?" Jacob asked.

"Yeah, sure. See you at noon at the track."

Clint wanted to go back to sleep but he couldn't. He was awake and wondering if *he* made the team or not.

The tension mounted throughout the day as Clint received several text messages and two calls from other guys saying the coach had paid them a visit. He was genuinely excited for each of them, but his anxiety was growing.

He went to the track as promised.

"Hey, thanks for coming," Jacob said.

"No problem. I had already told my mom I wanted to run today."

"Have you heard from the coach?"

"No, nothing yet."

"I wouldn't sweat it, man. I'm sure you made the team."

"You know I've never played football before."

"You told me. But I don't think that matters to the coach. He's looking beyond your resume. He's looking at character, potential, and desire. You got this."

"Thanks. Let's run," Clint said.

"I think we should walk first, you know . . . my warm-up lap," Jacob smiled.

"For sure."

The two new friends walked and ran, mostly walked, for the next hour. They talked about the three fundamentals and how they could use them in life outside of football.

Clint said, "Man, this has been great. Thanks for suggesting it, but I need to get home."

"I agree. You need to be there when the coach shows up."

"I'll be there."

Clint went home and tried to study but couldn't. Then he tried to take a nap but couldn't. He just kept thinking about what an amazing week it had been and how much he wanted to be part of the team. Finally, it was time for dinner. Clint went downstairs but couldn't eat.

"Are you feeling okay?" Megan asked. "Do you have a fever?"

Clint wondered if this was something she learned at mommy training school. *She always asks if I have a fever.*

"No, I'm fine. Just not hungry." He went back to his room and decided to do something productive. He was intrigued by the coach's comments about how he and the others might use this experience to Win Every Day forever. His conversation with Jacob had further piqued his interest, so he decided to write down some of what they had discussed. But before he wrote his first idea, he fell asleep. The uncertainty of the day had taken its toll.

Suddenly, awakened by the doorbell, he looked at his clock—it was ten o'clock! His dad called out, "Clint, Coach is here."

Clint hit only about two of the steps as he bounded downstairs, unable to contain his relief. "Coach, it's great to see you!"

"Well, I'm sorry it is so late. I wanted to stop by and say congratulations, you made the team." Tom handed Clint a jersey with his name already on the back.

"Thanks, Coach!"

"Again, I'm sorry I am so late; I like to deliver the jerseys personally, and there is a reason you are my last stop."

Clint, still holding the jersey, turned it over and saw a star on the front shoulder, just left of the number. "What's this?"

"That's what I was about to tell you. The team voted you as one of the two captains. And because I think you and I share the belief that the best leaders put others first, I knew you would want to be my last stop for the day."

"I don't know what to say." Clint was literally speechless. "Thank you."

Megan was so proud she began to cry.

"Mom," Clint said, "I'm not going off to war." They all laughed.

"Can you come in and have a cup of coffee?" Blake asked.

"No, it's late, and my wife is expecting me. But I am looking forward to our next meeting—I think we're scheduled for next Saturday?"

"Yes, we are—looking forward to it!"

"Clint, thanks for your leadership. I'm thankful to have you on the team. See you Monday."

The two men shook hands, not beginning to imagine the impact this new friendship would have on both of them for years to come.

Leaders Needed

B lake was more fired up than ever to improve the execution of his entire team. He was convinced the ideas Tom was teaching Clint could have a tremendous impact in his organization. He had asked for Ashley to schedule a standing weekly meeting to discuss the way forward.

"Good morning, Ashley! How was the conference?"

"Outstanding. And your week?"

"You won't believe what happened last week." Blake proceeded to tell Ashley about Clint's tryouts. "It was really an orientation to the Fundamentals of Execution." Blake stopped short of telling Ashley what Tom believed about execution. He wanted to hear her thoughts first.

"I can tell you more about all that at a later date. What's the status of your proposal?" Blake asked.

"My team should have our preliminary draft in a week or two."

"Let's take a look at what you have, even in draft form, next Monday morning. Can we do that?"

"Yes. It may still be rough."

"No problem."

"I'm also interested in learning more about your coach's approach to execution. Some of the global best practices for execution come from the world of sports."

"When we meet next week, you can share your current thinking, and I'll be prepared to share what I've learned from Tom."

"Deal."

~

The next week, Clint continued to learn the kicking game. Lucky for him, his years of soccer were helpful.

On Saturday morning, Blake went to have breakfast with Tom.

"How was last week?" Tom asked.

"The highlight was you showing up with that jersey!" Blake said.

"You've raised an amazing young man. His leadership gift is strong. The team saw it almost instantly. I didn't tell Clint, but every kid, except one, voted for him as captain."

"All but one?"

"Yes, I'm assuming he didn't vote for himself." Tom grinned. "Thanks to you and Megan for modeling the right behaviors for him."

"Thanks. I've just tried to model for him what my dad taught me."

"I'm living in the same place," Tom said.

"How is your dad?"

"Declining."

"I'm sorry."

"How can I serve you today? I think you called this meeting," Tom said, wanting to change the subject.

"I did. First, I've been drilling Clint for information every night about your fundamentals. I would love to review what I've learned and ask a few follow-up questions."

"Go for it."

Blake quickly reviewed what he had gleaned from Clint along with a rough working definition for each fundamental. "How am I doing?"

"Good, so far," Tom said.

"Which of the fundamentals is most challenging?" Blake asked.

"All of them!" Tom insisted. "But I can still give you an answer: the first one is the most difficult."

"Can you elaborate?"

"Sure. All of us, the leaders and the players, have to decide: Will I Pursue Mastery today or something less? Mastery sounds awesome in theory, but in the moment, in the grind, we can have an extremely difficult time mustering the integrity to actually pursue it."

"Why do you use the term *integrity* in this context?"

"Living a life congruent with your stated beliefs and values is, for me, an integrity issue. Do I walk the talk? Do my actions align with my words? Does my life validate my values? This is what integrity is all about. I believe integrity in the moment is critical. Without it, all you have left is untapped potential.

"If I have learned anything over the years as a leader, it is this: I am the biggest obstacle to my success—not my team, not my circumstances, not my resources, not my geography, not even my competition. By the way, do you know who my real competition is?"

"Uh . . . the other high schools in our state?"

"Nope. Arrogance and complacency are my nemeses. I must beat them every single day to give the team any chance of winning."

Arrogance and complacency are my nemeses.

"I have more work to do on this one," Blake said.

"Work that you'll never finish—stay on it," Tom said. "Other questions?"

"I am really interested in the role of the coaches; I'm looking for the parallels for my leaders. What do your coaches do to help you guys Win Every Day?" Blake asked.

"They do so much!" Tom laughed. "The world may call them coaches, but my guys are leaders, and as you know, leadership is real work."

"I do know that, but based on what we said a moment ago, I'm wondering if my leaders, myself included, are doing what we need to do. We're certainly not executing at the levels you are shooting for. Have you learned any specific leadership behaviors related to execution that make a big difference?"

"Well, yes, there are three; each corresponds with one of the fundamentals. Let me draw it for you."

Tom grabbed a napkin and began to write as he described each behavior. He drew two columns— one he titled "Everyone" and the other, "Leaders." Under the "Everyone" column, he wrote the three fundamentals.

"Okay, let's start with Pursue Mastery. I think you understand what that means, but don't forget, I labeled this column 'Everyone,' so it applies to the coaches too. However, leaders have additional responsibilities here. Yes, we will Pursue Mastery, but we must also Coach for Life."

"I didn't see that coming," Blake said.

"Many football coaches just coach football," Tom said.

"Uh, okay. What's wrong with that?"

"Nothing really. It just creates a real opportunity for us. Simply stated, we want to teach the boys a lot more than how to win football games—we want to teach them how to win in life—that's why we Coach for Life."

"Give me an example," Blake said.

"I'll give you several. We want to teach them to lead, to learn, and to begin creating their own legacy."

"Legacy? They are just kids," Blake said.

"Think of it like a reputation. We ask every player to decide, 'What do you want to be known for?' Then we ask, 'What has to change to make your desire a reality?'"

"Anything else? As if that's not enough." Blake smiled.

"We also want to improve their work ethic to help them get through the hard times in life. I guess to sum it up, we want to help them build strong character that will serve them forever."

"Basically, you want to help them become better people," Blake summarized.

"Exactly. Our premise is simple: better people make better football players."

"Why do you do all that? It sounds like just coaching football for a bunch of kids would be hard enough."

"Well, for me, it just feels like the right thing to do. If all I did was win football games, I'm not sure how fulfilling that would be."

"Seriously? You've won fifteen state championships. Are you saying that's not fulfilling?"

"We have won some games, but fulfilling? I'm not sure. I'll tell you what I am thankful for: I've had an opportunity to impact several thousand young people during my career thus far . . . kids like Clint.

"But hey, don't think I'm just some do-gooder, I'm fully aware of the positive impact this idea of coaching for life has on our football program. This approach builds trust, respect, engagement, and extra effort. The more we care about the players, their *whole* life, the more they care about our football program."

"Okay," Blake said, scratching his head. "I'm really gonna have to think about how this idea might or might not work in my organization. Can we talk about how your coaches help with the second fundamental?"

"Yep. As you know, we've asked everyone to Own the Numbers, but leaders have an additional role: Focus on Process."

"Okay . . . ," Blake said slowly. "Tell me more."

"Here's what I know about your organization," Tom said. "What you are doing today is working."

"What's that mean?" Blake asked.

"Results, good or bad, don't just happen. The outcome is the output of the process. If you are producing broken widgets, it's a direct reflection of a broken process. Change the process, change the outcome. When the numbers aren't what you want, a leader needs to evaluate the process and systems you have in place to identify the root cause of the problem.

"If a player is not making his blocks consistently, we need to ask, 'Where has the process broken down?' Maybe it was in selection, fit for the role, training, coaching, communication, conditioning, measurement, or some combination of these."

"What if the player isn't really trying?" Blake asked.

"Good question! Maybe he's not a good fit for the team. That would be a question regarding our selection process. Or maybe he doesn't understand what is expected of him; maybe he's confused about what Pursue Mastery really means. Maybe he's fatigued, so that would raise questions about our conditioning process. All of these are process issues. The coach has to figure out what went wrong to allow someone to half-heartedly do his job."

"And then, I guess you need to fix the process?" Blake suggested.

"Sometimes."

"Not always? Why wouldn't you?"

"Sometimes the process is not at fault. From time to time, we discover the process is solid but we didn't follow it as prescribed. A few years ago, we had a new coach who didn't do the entire set of warm-up drills before practice. Two players were injured that day, in part, because he took a shortcut and didn't follow the process."

"Are shortcuts common?"

"No. When we see them, we have another conversation. The process is the process for a reason." Tom smiled. "The process creates consistency."

"I'm afraid we're not thinking enough about the process. I have a sinking feeling that stuff just happens. I know, I know. Before you say it, 'stuff just happens' is not a real process."

"Correct. If something is an important factor in your success, there needs to be a process."

Blake made a few notes and then asked, "Can we go back to Own the Numbers for a minute?"

"Sure."

"How much of Own the Numbers is about the past and how much is about the future?"

"That's an insightful question! We want to learn from the past, but we don't want to live there. When we all Own the Numbers, we will always see gaps or opportunities for improvement. That's what we're looking for! Our coaches are specifically charged with identifying and closing critical gaps. If leaders aren't careful, a scorecard will do nothing more than chronicle the past. We don't want historians—we want history makers."

"Again, where do the numbers come from?"

"Sometimes the coaches provide the metrics. As an example, the line coach provides the key numbers and the daily scorecard for the linemen based on their performance. Other times, the coaches will help a player establish his own metrics—usually we use a combination of coach-created and player-created metrics for each position.

"Here's the bottom line: The numbers *always* tell a story. The coach is ultimately responsible to help the player write a better story."

"Okay, thanks. Let's shift. The third leadership behavior must be associated with Help Others Win," Blake said.

"You are correct. And there are countless ways a leader can Help Others Win. However, as it relates to execution, the one activity that rises to the top of my list is Communicate Tirelessly."

"I know what that means . . . but what does that mean?" Blake asked a bit overwhelmed by all he had already learned so far. "Like do you mean daily?"

"Oh, no. Much more often—think multiple times an hour."

"You're kidding, right?"

"Absolutely not. If we are to be successful inculcating the fundamentals, we must talk about execution nonstop. We are in the execution business. When we execute better than the other team, we win. It is really that simple. You may have heard 'The challenge is to keep the main thing the main thing.'"

"I have," Blake said.

"The main thing is execution. *All* conversations about new players, weight training, dietary needs, sleep, new offensive schemes, defensive changes, or even which shoes to wear this weekend in the rain should help us improve our execution."

"So tirelessly really means constantly?" Blake asked.

"Yes, and more."

"What's more than constantly?"

"Communication is the oxygen of execution. Therefore, the message must be everywhere. You'll find it painted on the walls, printed on our water bottles and our shirts. We'll give little Win Every Day stickers to players for superior execution—they put them on their helmets. We'll have a bulletin board, both digital and old-school, to celebrate individual and team wins. We will have a team newsletter called *Win Every Day*. We even gave the players an app to track their progress and record their personal wins."

"I know. Clint showed it to me. Incredible!" Blake said, amazed at Tom's level of intentionality. "Can you tell me again why you do all of this?"

"Communication creates focus, and focus is essential for elite levels of execution."

Blake couldn't remember the last time he delivered a message focused on execution, other than the press release containing his apology for the company's recent debacle. "Any other communication advice I should know about?" he asked.

"Sure. A lot more. At every team meeting we will also highlight individuals who have demonstrated one or more of the fundamentals."

"Every meeting?"

"Sure."

"Is that hard?"

"Not if you are winning every day," Tom laughed. "We have scores of examples every single day."

"And finally, here's one of my favorites." Tom pulled a coin from his pocket about the size of a silver dollar and handed it to Blake.

"What's this?"

"It's a challenge coin. I made one for each member of the team and support staff."

"Where did this idea come from?"

As Tom described the origins of the coin, Blake saw "Win Every Day" and the three fundamentals on one side and the team logo on the other.

"This is really cool," Blake said.

"Yeah, I agree. We'll ask the team to carry it with them all the time. Don't mention it to Clint yet. I will give them out before the first game. I share this as just one more example of how we as leaders work to Communicate Tirelessly."

"That is unbelievable," Blake said.

"There is a direct correlation between the level of communication and the level of execution. It is critical we get this right," Tom concluded and slid the napkin he'd been scribbling on across the table toward Blake.

Win Every Day

Everyone	**Leaders**
Pursue Mastery	Coach for Life
Own the Numbers	Focus on Process
Help Others Win	Communicate Tirelessly

"May I have this?"

"Sure. But if you write a book, I want you to mention me in the acknowledgments," Tom laughed.

"I want to live this book more than I want to write it. Thank you!"

🏆 Game Plan

The next week, Ashley was eager to meet with Blake to discuss her team's implementation ideas.

"Good morning, Blake," she said with a huge smile. "I'm excited to talk with you today about our plans to improve execution across the organization!"

"Not half as excited as I am to hear them," Blake chuckled.

"And I want to hear about how your coach is attacking his execution challenges. I checked him out. Do you know he is one of the winningest coaches in the history of high school football?"

"I do. I'm thankful my son can be on his team. What have you got for us to look at today?"

"I have a few slides to talk you through," she said, handing Blake a short deck.

"I'm ready."

"First, the situation: Levels of execution are stagnant. The 'process is in control.' We are getting the outcomes our current systems, structure, and practices are capable of producing.

"To improve our outcomes, we will have to change some things. Our improvement plan will focus on three main areas:

"*Leadership.* We must declare war on the status quo and cast a vision for a preferred future.

"*Measurement.* We must identify key execution metrics for all critical roles and processes.

"*Culture.* We must enlist everyone and make execution part of every job description."

"Thanks. Sounds simple." Blake smiled.

"Simple is not easy," Ashley said and returned the smile.

"Got it. I do have a few questions," Blake said.

"Fire away."

"Who's responsible for execution?" Blake asked.

"Is that intended to be a trick question?" Ashley asked with a slight smile.

"No, not really. What do you think?"

"Leaders are responsible for the ultimate outcome. However, the frontline employee does the work—he or she executes or not. So, if pressed, I would say *both* leaders and team members are responsible for execution—that's why we have to ultimately change the culture."

"I agree. And so would Tom," Blake said.

"Here's my next question," he continued. "How do we translate your focus areas into improved execution? Don't get me wrong. I think you've identi-fied the right pressure points, but honestly, it sounds really academic."

"We thought you might say that." Ashley smiled. "Turn the page and you'll see our outline for deploy-ment. Can I talk you through this?"

"Sure," Blake said.

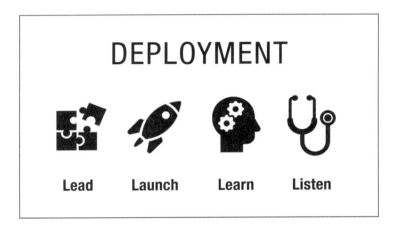

"Lead. As with virtually every significant change effort in the history of the world, it will have to start with leadership. Not just you and your team—but we'll have to align and enlist all our leaders."

"Yes, I can see why this is first. Tom acknowl-edges his coaches all have their own voice and perspective, but Win Every Day has to be their col-lective strategy. All the leaders have to sign up to run this play."

Ashley continued. *"Launch.* This is when the new strategy is revealed to the entire workforce. It's really a combination kickoff event and orientation."

"Good, this sounds similar to what Tom did during his tryouts. He took three afternoons to be sure the team understood the fundamentals."

"I don't think we'll take three days to do it, but this is a critical step in the process. If the team doesn't understand what we are doing, why it is important, and what we are asking them to do differently, we have no chance to Win Every Day," Ashley added.

"Learn," she continued. "This step represents all the individual conversations and applications that are necessary to make the core ideas come to life."

"Okay, what does that mean? If the core concepts were explained in the Launch phase, what is this?" Blake asked.

"This is where the ideas are translated into the real world. Let's use measurement as our example. It's fine to explain to people why measurement is important, even helpful to share a few examples, but what changes behavior and generates real, tangible results is when people are able to apply the concepts in *their* work. The Learn phase is when it all becomes personal.

"This phase of the transformation will involve many individual and team conversations. We'll help people answer questions such as, What numbers should I care about? What does owning those numbers really mean? How will my leader help me? These and other questions can't be answered in a launch event.

"And finally, *Listen*," Ashley said. "This, too, is critical. We will do our best to get this right from the beginning, but with history as our guide, we will not be perfect. We'll probably need to clarify some of our messages, modify some of our plans, and even change some of the ways we apply the concepts in our culture. Our process adjustments will be informed by what we hear from our people.

"Questions?"

"Not at the moment," Blake said.

"When do I get to hear what you've learned from the coach?"

"How about now?" Blake took the next few minutes to review the fundamentals with Ashley.

"Thanks, this is all very helpful. It sounds like Tom has given this a lot of thought."

"Thirty plus years in the execution business." Blake smiled. "What's next?"

"I want to share Tom's fundamentals with my team to see what they think about his language and overall approach."

"Great! I'll be sure we have time on the next executive team meeting agenda. Together, you and I will review the case for change and give an update on our progress."

~

Practices were going strong leading up to the first game. The team had picked up the plays quickly. Tom believed in a simple playbook. He was famous for saying, "If you execute well, you don't need a lot of plays."

If you execute well, you don't need a lot of plays.

Clint was the backup kicker and punter. Kyle was the starter and a good mentor for Clint.

The night of the first game, the coach's speech was simple: "We won yesterday in practice and the day before and the day before that. Let's do nothing different tonight. We Win Every Day!"

The visiting team was a former rival; however, since Tom had declared arrogance and complacency the only rivals, now they were simply the opposing team. Regardless, the returning players wanted to beat these guys to live down last year's humiliating defeat, 63–0.

At the end of the first quarter, the Falcon's, Tom's team, were up by a touchdown—and the same at halftime. The fans were on fire. The team was winning!

In the third quarter, the Falcons were up by two touchdowns. The place was going wild, but even from the stands, Blake noticed a concerned look on the coach's face as the fourth quarter began. Sure enough, the team began to sputter—they were running out of gas. On the first drive of the quarter, the other team scored with a lot of time left on the clock; the lead had been cut to seven.

Tom called run after run trying to bleed the clock. The strategy was working—until it wasn't. He found himself at fourth and six with three minutes to go. Kyle punted a good one, pinning the other team on their own five-yard line. Unfortunately, too much time was left and the Falcons were too tired to stop the other team. With ten seconds to go, the opposing team scored. A successful kick would tie the game, and a two-point conversion would win it.

The other coach, sensing his opponent's fatigue, decided to go for two. The game was over in a split second—the opponents scored; the Falcons lost. The final score: 29–28.

The Falcons' pain was real, but it was pain with purpose. For three quarters, the young team outexecuted their opponent. Then, they couldn't. The team decided right then that they would raise their level of intensity in the gym and on the practice field. They didn't want to ever run out of gas in the fourth quarter again.

Win Every Day

Ashley called Blake's office and asked for an additional meeting. Even though they were meeting weekly, she felt his urgency and wanted to be responsive.

"Thanks for squeezing in an extra meeting this week," Ashley said. "We've been looking at what Coach Moore has created. We think it captures really well what the best organizations in the world are doing. We want to adopt his language."

"I can support that direction. I was pleasantly surprised in our last meeting when your team's work aligned so well with his experience," Blake said.

"It really does underscore my team's belief that the principles and even the practices of world-class execution are universal and can be stated quite simply."

"That's comforting . . . I think." Blake paused.

"I sense some hesitation in your voice," Ashley noted.

"Yes, yes, you do."

"What are you thinking?"

"If the principles and practices are so *simple* and *universal*, why don't more organizations excel at execution?"

"Knowing a principle and executing on it are two entirely different animals," Ashley said.

"I'm listening."

"Let's choose an easy example: personal fitness. Everyone knows diet, exercise, and sleep are the keys to better health, energy, and productivity. However, the majority of Americans do not act on what they know."

"Why not?" Blake asked.

"I'm not a psychologist, but my assumption is there are tens of thousands of individual reasons, maybe millions. But the reasons and excuses don't nullify the truth about personal fitness. There are probably scores of reasons you and the leaders here have let our execution levels decline and stagnate. I'm not here to judge your past decisions. I am here, with help from Tom, to remind you that there is a better way forward. You can embrace the truth about execution or not; it will still be true."

"So, Win Every Day begins with a decision?"

"Yes, and to use Tom's language, will you Pursue Mastery?" She grinned.

"Good morning!" Blake said, addressing his team. "As you recall, Ashley joined us previously to share her assessment of the business. To recap, she asked us if we were good enough? I said no. Today, she is prepared to share her team's recommendations for how we can take our execution to elite levels. You may also recall she did extensive analysis to reach her conclusions regarding our current state. I asked her to begin her presentation today with a high-level review. Ashley, welcome back."

"Before she begins," Charles said, "what's our objective here today?"

"Our primary goal is to keep you informed. We'll also share some preliminary ideas regarding the way forward. After today, assuming we are aligned, we'll ask Ashley's team to build a detailed implementation plan.

"Any other opening comments or questions before we give the floor to Ashley?" Blake asked.

Kim, the unofficial second in command, spoke up. "First, I want to thank you, Ashley, for helping us see clearly what was right under our noses. I will say I have been guilty of being sucked into the quicksand of daily distractions. Certainly, our current level of execution is not good enough. These numbers do not represent our best efforts. We can do better."

"I agree," Jessica said, "and I like the thought about how higher levels of execution can impact the bottom line. I'm afraid to calculate the cost of poor execution. I'm guessing that number would be mind-blowing."

"Any other thoughts?" Blake said.

Sandeep said, "Do you guys realize how hard this is going to be? It's easy to look at a chart and say we can do better. But in reality, we have thousands of people doing millions of repetitive tasks. I'm not sure we have the leadership to pull this off. Sorry, Blake."

"I agree completely," Blake said. "Leadership will be required in massive doses, but you are correct: leadership *alone* will not create the change we want."

Leadership will be required in massive doses, but you are correct: leadership *alone* will not create the change we want.

"So if we want to change these numbers and the hundreds of others behind them, what do we have to do?" Roger asked.

"We have to involve everyone," Blake said. "Do you remember a few years ago when we spent time with Jack Deluca?"

A few nodded.

"Some of you were not here. He challenged us to build a high performance organization. We can review his ideas at a future meeting, but here's why I bring it up: Jack reminded us every organization is in a tug-of-war. He said the difference between high performance organizations and all the others is who you are pulling against: we want to be battling the competition and pulling together toward our goals, not pulling against our own team!

"This is our moment," Blake continued. "We need to get everyone on the same side of the rope—that's our job as leaders. And then, assuming we are aligned and the people fully engaged, we can excel at execution. We are going to need all hands on the rope to change these numbers!"

"Okay, based on our last meeting, I think we understand our current reality. What do you propose we do? Not metaphorically with a big rope—tomorrow, next week, next month, how do we move the numbers?" Sandeep's skepticism was showing.

It was now Ashley's turn. She referenced a slide containing the Win Every Day strategy.

☆ **Win Every Day** ☆

✔ **Pursue Mastery**

✔ **Own the Numbers**

✔ **Help Others Win**

Together, she and Blake spent about half an hour explaining each tenet and fielding questions.

"Any other big questions?" Blake asked.

Only Roger's hand went up. "I'm sorry, but my question is a variation of the one I asked a while ago. This is helpful and I can see how it would change this organization, but what do we do next?"

Ashley then shared the implementation outline and explained each element.

"Do we really have time to do this?" Sandeep said.

"Excuse me. What is your question?" Blake asked.

"Do we have time to put all this extra energy into execution?" he said.

Honestly, Blake was surprised by the question. He wondered if he had just discovered part of their problem. But he maintained his composure and said, "We do have a lot going on in the business. We are launching new products, expanding into new markets, working hard to recruit and retain top talent, and so much more. I know everyone is really busy. But here's my take on it: We are in the execution business. Our customers come to us with clear expectations—they want what they want the way they want it when they want it. Our job is to execute. All the activities of the enterprise should be focused on helping us meet customer expectations and demands. Execution is not one more thing—it is the thing. Have you forgotten about our recent social media fiasco? And then, there is the matter of our true competition."

"We're better than they are," groused Sandeep.

"That's exactly what I said in my first meeting with Ashley. And then I was troubled by my response. We said this topic of execution has a personal component. I had to wrestle with my own motivation and identity as a leader. With the help of a friend, I've changed my answer regarding the competition. Our competition is arrogance and complacency. If we can defeat these, we can Win Every Day."

Execution is not one more thing— it is the thing.

The thought about the "real competition" changed the tone in the room; Blake could see it on everyone's faces. Finally, he had struck a chord with his team. They were good leaders, perhaps trapped in the stress of the moment, but he knew they could escape and lead at a higher level.

"Next steps?" Blake asked.

"Here's my suggestion," Kim offered. "Let's ask Ashley to send us her *specific, detailed* recommendations—dates, costs, et cetera. We can put this on our next agenda in two weeks and make the final call."

🏆 Stronger

Over the next two weeks, Ashley and her team worked feverishly to have the detailed recommendations ready to send to the senior team in advance so they could prepare for the big meeting.

As it turned out, the meeting was unremarkable. This time, Blake presented the plan with Ashley there for moral support. The executives had very few questions and appeared genuinely optimistic, if not enthusiastic. All of them really did want to be part of something great, something remarkable. And they knew aligning and rallying hundreds of thousands of team members to this higher calling—a personal calling to Win Every Day—would make everyone involved a real winner. They would not only be stronger as an organization but be stronger as individuals.

The plan was adopted, and deployment meetings started the next week. A cross-functional team led by Ashley was formed and the process began. Senior leaders met with their leaders to begin cascading the message. Blake did an amazing job as he spoke to the entire staff. Tools and resources were created to help leaders communicate well, and people were recognized for helping others win. The best part: it was working! Within weeks, key execution metrics began to improve.

~

While Blake's team was growing stronger, so was Tom's. But not just physically—they were becoming stronger mentally and emotionally as well. This led to even higher levels of execution. Tom and his coaches asked the players to Win Every Day—literally every day.

They reminded the team of the three choices: "Will you Pursue Mastery today? Will you Own the Numbers? And will you Help Others Win?" The focus on execution was unrelenting.

The team won their next seven games, each by increasing point spreads. Even when the coaches put in the second- and third-string players to avoid running up the score, the team would continue to rack up points.

Then in the ninth game, a spot in the playoffs already secured, they hit a buzz saw—a team that appeared to have also decided to Win Every Day. These guys were really good. The Falcons knew after the first couple of plays that they would have their hands full. Nonetheless, they hung with the opposing team and the coach decided to let some guys play who hadn't seen a lot of game time.

In the fourth quarter with the score tied at 24–24 and seven seconds to go, the Falcons needed a field goal to win. Unfortunately, it would be a long one—forty-seven yards. Coach looked at Clint and said, "You got this."

Clint swallowed hard. He had never kicked a field goal from this distance in a game, and as he recalled, only once in practice had he made one this long.

"Yes, sir."

As the team broke the huddle, Clint looked to the sidelines and saw Kyle clapping and cheering for him.

The ball was snapped, the holder did his job, and Clint did what he had done thousands of times in practice: he kicked the ball in rhythm and with perfect form. Then, in what appeared to be slow-motion, both teams, the coaches, and the fans watched as the ball made its way toward the center of the goalposts on a perfect trajectory. It traveled end over end and landed on the crossbar, bounced straight up in the air, and fell to the ground on the wrong side of the bar. He had missed it!

As Clint's heart exploded with pain, he still had the presence of mind to *run* off the field. He thought he might try to avoid the coach but ran right into him. Before Clint could say anything, the coach said, "Great kick! Your form was perfect, you made really solid contact. I'm proud of you."

"But I missed it," Clint said, holding back his tears.

"Not really, it just didn't make it through the uprights. You did the right thing the right way; that's all any of us can ever do. We don't always control the outcomes, but we do control our effort. Now, let's go win this thing in overtime!" He slapped Clint on the back.

Much to Clint's surprise, as he met the rest of the team on the sidelines, they weren't mad at him either; they echoed Coach's encouragement. Clint knew he would remember this moment the rest of his life.

On the opponents' first possession in overtime, they were kept out of the end zone and they missed their field goal attempt.

The Falcons' first possession resulted in an uncharacteristic busted play in which they lost yards. Weighing his options, Tom decided to attempt a field goal. Once again, he sent Clint into the game. "Get this and let's go home—I'm hungry," the coach said with a smile.

This time, the kick was more manageable, a mere thirty-five yards. Clint knew if he hit the ball with the same stroke he had practiced fifteen minutes before, he would be good. He did—picture perfect—splitting the uprights, with plenty of room to spare.

The team went crazy. In the greater scheme of things, the game was inconsequential. They were headed to the playoffs anyway. But emotionally and psychologically, this game meant a lot.

The team dealt with adversity and disappointment and bounced back; they were reminded how important it is to stay focused; they also reaped the benefit of grit and tenacity. The missed field goal also allowed them to experience and practice what it really means to Help Others Win even under pressure.

The team went on to win easily in the first four rounds of the playoffs. Only the state championship game was left. All was good—almost. Tom's dad took a turn for the worse. He was hospitalized just days before the big game. As soon as Blake heard the news, he headed to the hospital.

As soon as Blake walked into the ICU, he saw Tom.

"Hey, man," Tom said. "What are you doing here? Shouldn't you be at work?"

"I'm here because you are! How's your dad?"

"Not good."

"What are they telling you?" Blake asked.

"Not much."

"Have you seen him?"

"Yes, he's lucid but really weak. I think this may be it for him."

"Anything you need to say? You've got that chance." Blake had a painful flashback to the unexpected death of his father. He had always wanted one more conversation.

"I know. I've been thinking about it."

"Is Lucy here yet?"

"No, I called her and the kids."

"I'll wait here for them. Go talk to your dad."

Tom agreed and walked past all the ICU rooms, each with a battery of machines fighting for the life they surrounded. There was a solemnity in the place that was palpable.

When he entered his dad's room, his dad was awake, staring at the ceiling. "Hello, son," he said in a hushed tone. "How are you?"

"I'm good, but a better question is, how are you?"

"Blessed," the old man said.

"Yes, Dad, we all are."

"What are the doctors telling you?"

"Not much, and you?"

"Nothing. How's prep for the big game coming?"

"You know the drill," Tom said.

"I do indeed. My guess is you have done nothing different for this game than the hundreds of others you've coached."

"You are correct. I'm just doing what you taught me."

The old man said, "The best way to win on game day is to . . ." He paused and coughed.

Tom finished his dad's sentence, "to Win Every Day."

"You know, that's why I have no regrets. Oh, I've not been perfect; your mom could have testified to that," his dad chuckled and coughed again. "I'm looking forward to seeing her soon. But I have no regrets because with God's help, I tried to Win Every Day. It wasn't the easy path, the most expedient, or even the most fun, but it was the right path."

"I know, Dad, you did. I have something for you." Tom pulled a challenge coin out of his pocket and placed it in his dad's hand.

"I created these for the team to remind us what you taught me."

"I like it," the old man said, slowly turning the coin in his hand.

"Son, you know how much I love you."

"I do."

"You know I'm proud of you."

"I do."

"Thanks for being the best son a father could ever have."

"You have been an amazing dad, friend, and mentor. I am so thankful for our life together."

"Son, it's fourth and goal for the last time, and I'm going to score." He smiled. "Please tell Lucy and the kids I love them. I'm going to rest now. I love you." He closed his eyes and was gone.

Tom sat by his bedside for several minutes. Amazing memories surged through his heart and mind. He hardly noticed the nurses and technicians who came within seconds to see what might be done to save his dad. Their well-intentioned efforts were in vain. He was really gone.

Tom walked out into the hallway and saw Lucy and the kids just coming into the waiting room.

"How is he?" Lucy asked.

"He's gone." A wave of emotions engulfed them. Huddled together, holding each other, they cried.

The funeral was on Saturday morning and the church was packed. The entire community showed up, including all the players and their families. The service celebrated a life so well lived, few tears were actually shed that day. More people left inspired than in mourning. However, many left the service with a sense of genuine regret that they had not known Tom's dad personally.

When the team assembled just a few hours later to board the buses, the coach was there with his game face on. He greeted the players as usual. Those outside the team wondered how Tom would hold up under the emotion of his situation. The players, having spent the season with him, knew he would do the right thing the right way.

In the pregame meeting, the coach stepped to the front of the room.

"Boys, thanks for showing up at my dad's memorial service. He was a great man—I hope you got a glimpse of that today. I want you to know he and I talked about this game in our last conversation. He expected us to do nothing differently than what we have done every day since tryouts last spring. Please don't think of this as the state championship game; this is just one more day in a long line of days. As you've heard me say hundreds of times, you have three choices to make: Will you Pursue Mastery? Will you Own the Numbers? Will you Help Others Win? Your choices are the only things you can control. Choose wisely.

Your choices are the only things you can control. Choose wisely.

"Some of you may be tempted to win tonight for me or my dad. Don't fall in that trap. Win today because it is what you do every day. We will do the right thing the right way every time to the best of our abilities. We will leave this field in three hours with no regrets—regardless of the score. When you Win Every Day, you can live a life with no regrets . . . oh, and don't forget—have fun!"

Beyond the emotions of the day, the team did have one additional variable to deal with: the temperature. It was seven degrees at kickoff. None of the boys had ever played in these conditions.

Both teams were talented, well coached, and evenly matched. At halftime the score was 14–14. At the end of the third quarter, 21–21. Then with twenty-seven seconds to go, Kyle kicked a thirty-nine-yard field goal to give the Falcons the lead.

As the team came running off the field, Kyle stopped and grabbed the back of his leg. He let out a yell and fell to the ground. The pain was excruciating—he was down on the frozen turf unable to get up. Kyle had pulled his hamstring.

As the team huddled on the sidelines for the kickoff, Tom looked at Clint: "Kick it deep," he said, grinning.

As Clint stood over the ball, he reviewed his responsibilities. He had practiced kickoffs a lot but had never done one in a game. When the official gave the signal, Clint kicked the ball as high and as far as he could. The ball was fielded on the three yard line by the fastest player on the other team. He was like lightning. He made the first two guys miss and then he reversed field. Then he hurdled a would-be tackler and reversed field again. He had only one guy to beat before reaching midfield, and he did! Only Clint was left to make the tackle. He chose his angle and ran like he had never run before, hitting the runner just after he crossed the fifty-yard line and knocking him out of bounds.

Only seven seconds remained on the clock. Thanks to Clint's heroics, the opponents were out of field goal range. They would have only one play, and everyone knew it would be a Hail Mary.

The ball was snapped. The quarterback dropped back and threw the ball as far as he could—a mass of players all leaped for the ball. It was the quietest anyone had ever heard a stadium full of people. And in the midst of the mayhem on the field, the wide receiver caught the pass! Clint and the others on the sideline were in shock. But the receiver fell on the two-yard line, short of the end zone. The whistle blew. The game was over. The Falcons had won!

🏆 Legacy

Tom and Blake were scheduled to meet at their usual spot on the Saturday after the big game.

"What an emotional week—first, your dad, then, the game. How are you holding up?" Blake began.

"Okay, I guess. One thing I've tried to do over the years is to manage the peaks and valleys. If I can maintain the right perspective, it helps. I'm trying to teach the boys that too."

"Clint is getting it. Thanks for the influence you've already had on him—not just as a player but as a human being."

"You know, Clint is a special young man—you've created a wonderful legacy."

"I didn't start it, but I am trying to continue it. Like with you, my dad got the ball rolling. I'm just trying to steward his legacy," Blake said.

"I owe you a huge thank-you," Tom said.

"For what?"

"For encouraging me to talk with my dad. Had I not done that, I would be living with heartbreaking regret. Thank you!

"I have a gift for you," Tom said.

"For me? What are you talking about?"

Tom reached into his pocket and pulled out a challenge coin. "I showed this to you at the beginning of the season." He handed the coin to Blake.

"I remember."

"We made two extra ones. I gave one to Dad, and this last one is for you."

"Thanks," Blake said. "This means more to me than you can imagine. Our time together and the ideas on this coin have helped me get my leadership and my organization back on track!"

"How are things at work?"

"We're making progress. We've started using a common language regarding execution, and our numbers are improving."

"Congratulations!"

"Thanks! What's next for you?" Blake asked.

"Same as yesterday, the day before, and the day before that—all I'm trying to do is Win Every Day!"

"Me too."

Acknowledgments

As I referenced in the introduction, the amount of work behind this book was significant. Unfortunately, the simple style of a business fable is often misconstrued as a sign of little rigor and insight. These acknowledgments should validate the amount of time, energy, effort, and financial resources we invested on your behalf. Regarding insights, we trust you found at least a few to help you on your journey to high performance.

As you know from experience, execution at the levels we are advocating is extremely rare. The primary reason: it is *really* hard! Not only are elite levels of execution difficult, but to discern and distill the universal principles into something approachable for leaders around the world is daunting. The only reason you have access to this information today is the extraordinary team who worked behind the scenes for years to bring this content to life. I want to recognize some of them here.

To the core team who traveled, trained, coached, interviewed, debated, argued, pushed, challenged, and, in some cases, prayed for wisdom and clarity, thank you! Although the lines were often blurred, with some of the women and men listed below wearing multiple hats, the work fell into several primary categories. I'll start there:

Research—Discovering and synthesizing all the world knows about execution may sound like an impossible task. Not to this team! Their historical perspective on global best practices combined with their ethnographic skills and insights created the foundation for this book. Thank you, Michael Barry, Michelle Jia, Sonia Baltodano, Virginia Rath, Ryan Wolff, and Sara Beckman. Thanks also to the leaders who opened their organizations to help us learn about the topic of execution. Your contributions were immeasurable!

Content Development—On this project, research was foundational, but someone needed to translate what we learned and be sure it would stand the test of the real world. The following men and women were unrelenting in their efforts to help leaders know with confidence how to Win Every Day. Thanks to Randy Gravitt, Greg Hall, Chris Burzminski, Imran Jiwani, Erin Myers, Tony Gardner, Cameron Gilchrist, Jessica Everett, Mike Fleming, Steve Dull, Drew Brannon,

Milt Lowder, Jack Lannom, Steven Thorson, Gina Tucker, Bob Garrett, Dean Sandbo, Tim Tassopoulos, and Cliff Robinson. Without your wise counsel, this book, and the elite levels of execution it enables, would still be out of reach for most of the leaders in the world.

Training—After we had a point of view, we wanted to test it. To do that, we created two training events. The team created amazingly effective learning environments for leaders to understand what has to happen on the front lines to Win Every Day. Thanks to Jeff Docherty, Eliza Robson, Allison Craig, Rob Gomez, Sara Hopkins, Monica Banks, Justina Hunter, Haylee Sams, and Conniece Wilkins. You set a high bar for future events!

Coaching—After the training, the leaders we trained went back into the whirlwind. They had businesses to run, customers to serve, and problems to solve. Our coaches listened, shared best practices, and challenged more than seventy business leaders to Win Every Day. Thanks to Scott Morgan, Bonnie Wozniak, Jodi Wozniak, Chuck Cusumano, Scott Barber, and Steve Spoelhof. You guys reminded me once again why a coach is essential for men and women who want to reach their full potential.

Validation—Finally, the leaders from around the country who field-tested our ideas in multiple phases over the last two years deserve much praise. Thanks to the following for your patience, insight, and challenges as we slogged our way to our final conclusions; most importantly, thanks for your personal commitment to Win Every Day: Brent Allen, Daniel Andrews, Alex Aviles, Jeff Bassett, Chris Beckler, Ashley Bellamy, Erik Benitez, Pat Braski, Niel Brown, Chad Burn, Stew Butler, Colby Cameron, David Chen, David Clark, Roger Clark, Karen Colley, Craig Craddock, Chris Darley, Nicki Digby-Dalton, Jason Dittman, Chris Eckert, Robert Eike, Ignacio Eraso, Robert Ervin, Andrew Farr, Curt Flournoy, Steven Franklin, Natasha Gilbert, Danny Goepp, Barrie Goettsche, Don Gonzalez, Brian Goode, David Grossnickle, Eddie Halliday, Micah Harris, Wayne Hassler, Brian Heberlie, Robert Hewes, Brian Hilgenfeld, Jude Hodges, Megan Jacques, Bill Johnson, Eddie Kober, Dawn Kosir, Javier Laguna, Steve LaVoye, Michel Lusakueno, Frieda Marroquin, Steve Miller, Justin Mize, Daniel Moore, Jeff Mosley, Todd Murgi, Jamerian Myles, James Novak, David Oakes, Anthony Piccola, Jonathan Pickett, Ted Reim, David Roberts, Ryan Saxby, Devon Scanlon, Britt Sims, Joette Smith, Tate Smith, Kyle Steck, Jeremy Tatman, C. T. Taylor, Rob Taylor, K. J. Wari, Randy Watson, Aaron Weast, Joe Weber, Mike Weeks, and Josh Wynn.

Communications—No effort of this magnitude is sustainable without intentional, strategic communications. We were reminded of this truth when we didn't do so well during our first phase of this work. My apologies to the participants of Pilot #1. Thankfully, we found some professionals to help us in Pilot #2! Thanks to Lane Chalfant, Jessica Merrill, Jillian Broaddus, Caleb Stanley, and Kyle Delk. Communication is the oxygen of execution!

Publishing and Editorial—As usual, Berrett-Koehler showed up in a big way; Steve Piersanti led his team well! Thanks to Donna Miller, Janice Rutledge, Sarah Jane Hope, and Ken Fracaro for reviewing and improving the manuscript. Thanks to Valerie Caldwell, Irene Morris, and Lindsay Miller for their design expertise. Peter Hobbs, thanks for bringing the cover to life with your wonderful photography. And finally, Sharon Goldinger, thank you for providing the finishing touches on the manuscript. I would have loved to have you as a teacher the first time I was supposed to learn grammar and punctuation!

∼

Another callout is in order—Ari Zachas has worn many hats during this project. He has been thought partner, analyst, content creator, researcher, coach, measurement guru, and champion for the cause of execution. Thank you, Ari!

A special thanks to Jessica Hampton. The amount of administrative work behind this multiyear quest was staggering. She was the glue that held all the various pieces together. Thank you!

And finally, to the hundreds of thousands of employees in the scores of organizations we studied and those within the businesses who tested these concepts, thank you. We know your hard work is what really enables an organization to Win Every Day.

About the Author

Mark Miller is a business leader, best-selling author, and communicator.

Mark started his Chick-fil-A career working as an hourly team member in 1977. In 1978, he joined the corporate staff working in the warehouse and mail-room. Since that time, he has provided leadership for Corporate Communications, Field Operations, Quality and Customer Satisfaction, Training and Development, Leadership Development, and more. During his tenure with Chick-fil-A, the company has grown from seventy-five restaurants to over twenty-five hundred locations with annual sales exceeding $12 billion.

He began writing almost twenty years ago when he teamed up with Ken Blanchard, coauthor of *The One Minute Manager*, to write *The Secret: What Great*

Leaders Know and Do. The book you now hold in your hand is his ninth. With over one millon books in print, in more than twenty-five languages, Mark's global impact continues to grow.

In addition to his writing, Mark enjoys encouraging and equipping leaders. Over the years, he's traveled to dozens of countries teaching for numerous international organizations.

Mark is also an avid photographer who loves shooting in some of the most remote places on the planet. Past adventures have taken him to the jungles of Rwanda in search of silverback gorillas, across Drake Passage to Antarctica, across the equator to the Galapagos Islands, to the summit of Kilimanjaro, and to Everest Base Camp.

Mark has been married to Donna, his high school sweetheart, for over thirty-five years. They have two sons, Justin and David, a daughter-in-law, Lindsay, and three amazing grandchildren, Addie, Logan, and Finn.

Mark would love to connect with you:

Web: TMarkMiller.com
Instagram: TMarkMiller
Twitter: @LeadersServe
Linkedin: Mark Miller
Cell: 678-612-8441

Additional Resources

Win Every Day Field Guide

If you've read any of my books or other business fables before, you understand the limitations of the genre. My publisher reminds me often, "Your books are intended to introduce an idea—you are not writing a field guide." Several years ago, after I was asked to remove about 75 percent of the content from a manuscript, I decided to actually write a field guide. This has now become part of my standard publishing process. So, if you are looking for scores of tactics, case studies from other organizations, assessment questions, meeting agendas, and more, the *Win Every Day Field Guide* is your resource. My coauthor, Randy Gravitt, and I we have attempted to give you all the information you'll need to put the ideas you've just read into practice.

Win Every Day Quick Start Guide

After we had been producing Field Guides for sev-

eral years, some of our leaders asked for a new and different resource. The conversation went something like this: "The Field Guides are great—Please keep creating them. But something is missing." Obviously, this comment got our attention. After much discussion and inquiry, we decided what was "missing" was a resource for frontline leaders. Although the Field Guide contained all the information needed, it was too cumbersome and honestly too much for frontline leaders. So, we created the Quick Start Guide. It's a pocket-sized booklet focused on daily application. Each key concept is represented in a few paragraphs and the balance contains specific, tangible action steps a frontline leader can take to begin implementing the ideas from the book. The feedback has been so positive, we've gone back and created Quick Start Guides to support the entire High Performance Series.

Win Every Day Implementation Plan—Free PDF

I realize the implementation outline Ashley shared with Blake was really thin—due to constraints imposed by the medium. However, if you want a more detailed implementation plan, you can go to WinEveryDayBook.com/resources and we'll send you a FREE PDF. The plan will certainly need to be modified based on your situation, but I believe it will be helpful.

Other Books and Resources

As you may know, I've had the opportunity to write several books and supplemental resources over the last twenty years. If you need books, Field Guides, Quick Start Guides, assessments, and more, you can go to LeadEveryDay.com. As long as I have a day job, my profits will be donated to charity.

Keynotes, Training, and Coaching

I receive countless calls about coaching and training built around the content of my books. However, I still sell chicken for a living. This is good for me but doesn't help you with the challenges of implementing the ideas in this book. So, in an effort to help, I've certified some coaches, trainers, and communicators. If you are interested, you can go to TMarkMiller.com and find the Services tab. There you'll find folks who can assist you.

Also Part of the High Performance Series

Win the Heart
How to Create a Culture of Full Engagement

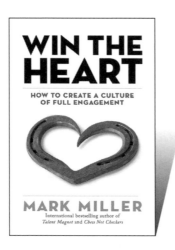

Every great company has an engaged workforce, and nurturing a culture of engagement is at the heart of great leadership—employees who really care about their work, their coworkers, and the organization can supercharge a company's success. Mark Miller draws on more than forty years of leadership experience to show leaders at all levels how to change the conversation and create real competitive advantage in the process. If you put the lessons in this book to work, your people will never look at work, or their leaders, the same way again.

Hardcover, 160 pages, ISBN 978-1-5230-9987-0
PDF ebook, ISBN 978-1-5230-9988-7
ePub ebook, 978-1-5230-9989-4
Digital audio, 978-1-5230-9991-7

Berrett–Koehler Publishers, Inc.
www.bkconnection.com   **800.929.2929**

Also Part of the High Performance Series

Talent Magnet
How to Attract and Keep the Best People

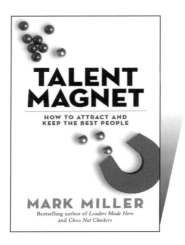

In *Talent Magnet*, Blake Brown, a CEO, is struggling to win the war for talent. At the same time, his sixteen-year-old son, Clint, is looking for his first job. These parallel stories surface insights from both the organization's perspective and the fresh eyes of top talent. The concepts in this book are based on extensive research and give you the tools to attract and retain top talent.

Hardcover, 144 pages, ISBN 978-1-5230-9495-0
PDF ebook, ISBN 978-1-5230-9496-7
ePub ebook, ISBN 978-1-5230-9497-4
Digital audio, ISBN 978-1-5230-9499-8

Berrett–Koehler Publishers, Inc.
www.bkconnection.com   **800.929.2929**

Also Part of the High Performance Series

Leaders Made Here
Building a Leadership Culture

Great leaders create great organizations. However, a scarcity of leaders today means a shortfall in performance tomorrow. Don't gamble with your company's future!

Mark Miller describes how to nurture leaders throughout the organization, from the front lines to the executive ranks. *Leaders Made Here* outlines a clear and replicable approach to creating the leadership bench every organization needs.

Hardcover, 144 pages, ISBN 978-1-62656-981-2
PDF ebook, ISBN 978-1-62656-982-9
ePub ebook, ISBN 978-1-62656-983-6
Digital audio, ISBN 978-1-62656-985-0

Chess Not Checkers
Elevate Your Leadership Game

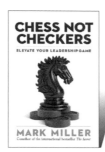

The early days of an organization are like checkers: a quickly played game with mostly interchangeable pieces. But as the organization expands, the same old moves won't cut it anymore. You have to think strategically, plan ahead, and leverage every employee's specific talents—that's chess. Mark Miller outlines four essential strategies that will transform your leadership and your organization!

Hardcover, 144 pages, ISBN 978-1-62656-394-0
PDF ebook, ISBN 978-1-62656-395-7
ePub ebook, ISBN 978-1-62656-396-4
Digital audio, ISBN 978-1-62656-603-3

Berrett–Koehler Publishers, Inc.
www.bkconnection.com   **800.929.2929**

The Heart of Leadership
Becoming a Leader People Want to Follow

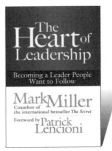

In this enlightening and entertaining business fable, Mark Miller identifies the five unique character traits exhibited by exceptional leaders. When Blake Brown is passed over for a promotion, he is sent on a quest to meet with five of his late father's colleagues, each of whom holds a piece of the leadership puzzle. This book shows us that leadership needn't be the purview of the few—it is within reach for millions around the world.

Hardcover, 144 pages, ISBN 978-1-60994-960-0
PDF ebook, ISBN 978-1-60994-961-7
ePub ebook, ISBN 978-1-60994-962-4

The Secret of Teams
What Great Teams Know and Do

What separates teams that really deliver from the ones that simply spin their wheels? In this book, executive Debbie Brewster learns from three very different teams—the Special Forces, NASCAR, and a local restaurant. Debbie and her team discover the three elements that all high-performing teams have in common, how to change entrenched ways of thinking and acting, how to measure your progress, and more.

Hardcover, 144 pages, ISBN 978-1-60994-093-5
PDF ebook, ISBN 978-1-60994-109-3
ePub ebook, ISBN 978-1-60994-110-9

Berrett–Koehler Publishers, Inc.
www.bkconnection.com   800.929.2929

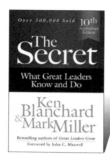

Dear reader,

Thank you for picking up this book and welcome to the worldwide BK community! You're joining a special group of people who have come together to create positive change in their lives, organizations, and communities.

What's BK all about?

Our mission is to connect people and ideas to create a world that works for all.

Why? Our communities, organizations, and lives get bogged down by old paradigms of self-interest, exclusion, hierarchy, and privilege. But we believe that can change. That's why we seek the leading experts on these challenges—and share their actionable ideas with you.

A welcome gift

To help you get started, we'd like to offer you a **free copy** of one of our bestselling ebooks:

www.bkconnection.com/welcome

When you claim your **free ebook**, you'll also be subscribed to our blog.

Our freshest insights

Access the best new tools and ideas for leaders at all levels on our blog at ideas.bkconnection.com.

Sincerely,

Your friends at Berrett-Koehler